THE LOST
DREAM

STEVE SIMMONS

THE LOST DREAM

The Story of Mike Danton, David Frost, and a Broken Canadian Family

VIKING
CANADA

VIKING CANADA

Published by the Penguin Group

Penguin Group (Canada), 90 Eglinton Avenue East, Suite 700, Toronto, Ontario, Canada M4P 2Y3
(a division of Pearson Canada Inc.)

Penguin Group (USA) Inc., 375 Hudson Street, New York, New York 10014, U.S.A.
Penguin Books Ltd, 80 Strand, London WC2R 0RL, England
Penguin Ireland, 25 St Stephen's Green, Dublin 2, Ireland (a division of Penguin Books Ltd)
Penguin Group (Australia), 250 Camberwell Road, Camberwell, Victoria 3124, Australia
(a division of Pearson Australia Group Pty Ltd)
Penguin Books India Pvt Ltd, 11 Community Centre, Panchsheel Park, New Delhi – 110 017, India
Penguin Group (NZ), 67 Apollo Drive, Rosedale, Auckland 0632, New Zealand
(a division of Pearson New Zealand Ltd)
Penguin Books (South Africa) (Pty) Ltd, 24 Sturdee Avenue, Rosebank, Johannesburg 2196, South Africa

Penguin Books Ltd, Registered Offices: 80 Strand, London WC2R 0RL, England

First published 2011

All efforts have been made to locate the permission holders for all of the images. All photographs except for
that of the Frost cottage provided by Steve and Sue Jefferson. Frost cottage photograph by Joe Warmington.

1 2 3 4 5 6 7 8 9 10 (RRD)

Manufactured in the U.S.A.

LIBRARY AND ARCHIVES CANADA CATALOGUING IN PUBLICATION

Simmons, Steve, 1957-
    The lost dream : how NHL ambition destroyed one Canadian family / Steve Simmons.

Includes index.
ISBN 978-0-670-06529-5

1. Danton, Mike, 1980–. 2. Frost, David, 1967–. 3. Jefferson family. 4. St. Louis Blues (Hockey team)—
Biography. 5. Hockey players—Canada—Biography. I. Title.

GV848.5.D33S54 2011   796.962092   C2011-903929-X

Visit the Penguin Group (Canada) website at **www.penguin.ca**

Special and corporate bulk purchase rates available; please see
www.penguin.ca/corporatesales or call 1-800-810-3104, ext. 2477.

To Sheila, Jeffrey, and Michael,
who make all my dreams possible

To Jody, the brother i lost too soon
and never knew or understood

CONTENTS

Preface   ix

1   Life, Death, and the Stanley Cup Playoffs   1

2   Young Mike and Minor-Hockey Life   17

3   Frost Warnings   27

4   Tom's Story   43

5   Mom's Story   61

6   Dad's Story   79

7   "The Most Powerful Man in Hockey"   99

8   Junior Daze   119

9   Draft Day and the Disappearing Dad   133

10   The Christmas Treatise   143

11   The Agent Who Couldn't Let Go   147

12   *The People vs. David Frost*   175

13   Guilt without Explanation   195

14   Second Chances   215

15   The Last Conversation   233

Postscript   249

Acknowledgments   251

Index   257

In the summer of 2002, at the tender age of 21, Michael Stephen Jefferson, a little-known professional hockey player, legally changed his name to Michael Sage Danton, ostensibly divorcing himself from his biological family.

His parents, Steve and Sue Jefferson, were never informed of the name change. They learned about it the way they learned about much of the rest of Mike's hockey-playing career and life: They read about it in the newspapers. To this day, the Jeffersons, including younger brother Tom, remain heartbroken, discouraged, and shattered over the change of name and all that has happened, real and imagined, to cause it.

That same summer, Mike's hockey mentor and surrogate father, David Frost, was certified as a player agent by the National Hockey League Players' Association. Those changes, first of one's name, then of the other's title, may have seemed insignificant and unimportant at the time, except to the Jefferson family. But both these men, in their chosen professions of hockey player and hockey agent, would soon become well known and not necessarily for the right reasons.

This book is not just Mike Danton's and David Frost's story, and they have not participated in most of the fact gathering here. Primarily, this is the story of a fragmented family and the circumstances surrounding a hockey dream gone wrong. There is some language here that is graphic and that may offend some. There are parts of this story that may be difficult to comprehend and digest. For that, I apologize in advance.

It would be impossible to try to tell this story any other way.

—*Steve Simmons, 2011*

Life, Death, and the Stanley Cup Playoffs

All his life, Mike Jefferson wanted nothing more than to play professional hockey. It was his passion, his obsession, his identity. It defined the odd life that he lived. He was a hockey player, first and foremost. Not a strategist. Not a deep thinker. Not even a very mature young man. He was a hockey player in the Stanley Cup playoffs for the very first time and what could be better than that?

This is, after all, the stuff dreams are made of. Kids and Canada and hockey. It is our game, our dream. We have all seen those Stanley Cup moments of elation. They're on television every June, on commercials every spring. In our minds, and on our driveways and backyard rinks, we have all scored that big playoff goal, those of us culturally and recreationally attached to hockey. We have all, in our thoughts, skated out on the ice for that first playoff game, with the crowd chanting our name, the noise blaring, the arena full of anticipation and excitement.

We may have dreamed it: Mike Jefferson, under a new name, lived it. It is remarkable for any kid from a bedroom community north and west of Toronto, or anywhere for that matter, to make it this far in professional hockey, to make a name for himself and have it stitched on the back of an NHL sweater. It's all the more remarkable for that kid to be lacing up his skates come playoff time. It is what he plays for, lives for as an athlete. Making the NHL is an against-all-odds proposition in the first place, especially when your talent doesn't come easily, when your size doesn't cast a shadow quite as long as your teammates', when your skill doesn't match up against that of your opponent. But there was something inside Mike Jefferson, something not easily defined—a purpose, a tenacity, an energy, an unmatched will—that brought him to the best hockey league in the world.

That took him to the Stanley Cup playoffs for the very first time.

Easter weekend 2004 should have been the best time of Mike Jefferson's young hockey life, except he wasn't Mike Jefferson any more. Two years earlier, he had changed his name to Mike Danton, divorcing himself from the family he grew up in, bringing more attention to a career that would have been better off with less. Having chosen the company of his agent, mentor, coach, and surrogate father, David Frost, over that of his own father, Steve, his own mother, Sue, and his own younger brother, Tom, made him infamous before he was about to become famous. The name Danton was picked pretty much out of a hat—he borrowed it from a kid he had met years before at hockey school. The timing of the name change, however, was anything but coincidental. It corresponded with Frost being certified as a player agent by the National Hockey League Players' Association. Jefferson took a name; Frost garnered a new title. They both became famous, in a hockey world sort of way, but for none of the reasons either of them would ever see coming.

"Hey Ronnie, it's Mike Danton calling ..."

Danton's St. Louis Blues were playing the impressive San Jose Sharks in their April 2004 first-round playoff series. Danton's job for the Blues was very simple: he was there to play the pest and unnerve the Sharks. He was to get under the skin of his opponents and try to distract them by saying things, doing things, keeping San Jose players on edge. And if all else failed, under the right game circumstances, he was there to fight.

That was the job description. You do whatever it takes to win. If it meant saying something you didn't want to say, you said it without any kind of remorse. If it meant using your stick as a weapon, you used it. If it meant, in Danton's case, acting like you were crazed, like you were capable of doing anything, you played that role, wanting to keep people on edge. It works best when even your own team doesn't know what you will do next. That's part of the job, being unpredictable, doing something to alter a game that no one else is willing to do. You don't just keep your opponent on guard, you keep your team on guard. And on every team in pro hockey, there is a certain quiet regard and respect for the player taking on that uncomfortable role.

"When he was on the ice, you knew it," said Ron Wilson, the Sharks' coach at the time, when looking back at that 2004 playoff series. "You always had to keep an eye on him because you weren't sure what he was going to do. The guys on our team were talking about him. He was doing his job. He was acting a little goofy. I know some of the guys on our team thought he was kind of crazy. He was saying crazy things. Doing crazy things. I know some of the guys in our dressing room were talking about him a lot."

Neither team, however, had any idea of how lethally unpredictable

Mike Danton really was throughout the five-game, eight-night, playoff series against the Sharks.

Normally, an athlete in a playoff series isn't just asked to be all in. It's *demanded* of him. The intensity is extreme. It's not just about the game and the strategy involved. It's about preparation. It's about playing a role. It's about getting maximum performance from every player on every successful team. It's about teams growing closer together. There are few shortcuts. Playoff hockey can be, and usually is, all-consuming—from team practices, to meetings, to morning skates, to video sessions, to airplane flights, to team meals. It takes over a player's life, with almost every minute of every day planned out and predetermined.

Playoff hockey is almost an entirely different game than regular-season hockey. It is played at a higher speed, with more intensity and more at stake. You have to give more of yourself in the post-season. The injured play hurt. Players are expected to make and take hits they wouldn't bother with during the season. You are told to throw your body in front of pucks you likely would have avoided in November. This is the hockey version of cranking up the sound on your stereo, almost to inaudible levels—sport on fast-forward.

"The way Mike was playing, you would never have known something else was going on with him," said Larry Pleau, general manager of St. Louis from 1997 to 2010, the man who acquired Danton to play for the Blues. "You're so focused as a general manager on what's going on, you can't conceive that something else might be. You just don't think that way. We knew when we traded for Mike that he came with some baggage, that he had some history. We knew about it and made it our business to monitor what was going on with him. We would talk about that often. We thought we were succeeding and honest, we thought we were doing a good job with him, and he was doing a good job for us."

On Easter Sunday, the day before St. Louis would play host to its first Stanley Cup playoff game that spring, the first home playoff game of Danton's career, Mike picked up his cellphone and dialled 618-971-8149. This was not your everyday pre-game preparation. He was calling Ronnie Jones. The two men had met a month earlier at a strip club in East St. Louis that Danton frequented, where Jones was employed as a bouncer. You wouldn't call what they had a friendship, but Jones knew who Danton was, and Danton was aware of who Jones was. Or, at least, he thought he was aware of who he was.

He thought Jones was a professional hit man.

In the midst of the Stanley Cup playoffs, in the intensity of all that, Mike Danton called Ronnie Jones and offered to pay him to murder his agent, David Frost.

He made that shocking call on Easter Sunday, according to the FBI, even though Jones had previously told Danton he wouldn't do the work. They had talked about this before the playoffs began. Apparently Jones turned down the hit, not because the $10,000 Danton had offered wasn't enough. He said no, he claims, because if he had ever been in the business of killing, which he didn't say he was, he certainly wasn't in that business any more.

Some of this is still so hard to believe and understand, even all these years after the fact. It is one thing to make the NHL, another to get to the playoffs, another to see your career so close to blossoming. And in the midst of an all-consuming experience, the most consumed hockey player anyone knew, Mike Danton, couldn't get his mind off David Frost.

Playoffs here, murder there. How could you make sense of any of it? Danton wanted the man he was closest to in the world gone from his life. Dead. And he was desperate enough to want it done right away.

It wasn't a passing thought. He had been thinking about it for months. Plotting the death of Frost. And when Mike Danton called Ronnie Jones on Easter Sunday—and Jones knew what the call was about—the bouncer chose not to answer the phone. He allowed it to go to message. He wanted no part of what was to come. Earlier, Danton had met with him at the bar and approached him about the possibility of "taking care" of Frost. He gave Jones a photograph of his agent. He cited a dispute over money he was having with Frost.

The telephone calls to Ronnie Jones seemed drastic enough, as the FBI transcripts taken from Jones's phone reveal. They all came between Game 2 and Game 3 of the Blues–Sharks playoff series. Their Easter Sunday conversation:

"It's twelve o'clock Sunday afternoon," Danton said on Jones's phone. "Hope things went well with your boy. Let me give you my schedule for the next two days. Probably won't be able to give you a shout later on today. Just wanted to let you know that he's [Frost] there now at my place. My schedule Monday and Tuesday, we play home games. I leave the house at nine in the morning. I have pre-game skate at 10:30 both Monday and Tuesday, so he'll be there like between nine and twelve. So that would probably be the best time.

"You know the details about what we talked about before, and uh, ya know, you know, I'll give you a call tomorrow morning. Leave your cellphone on so I can call you. Try to call you later today but I doubt I'll be able to. But hope you can hook me up, man. Like I said, I'll make it worth your while.... Talk to you tomorrow morning. All right, buddy. You've got my address: 1800 South

Brentwood Boulevard. It's off 46 or off 464. Apartment 1382, Villas of Brentwood. All right, buddy. I'll talk to you tomorrow. Leave your cell on so I can grab ya."

Ronnie Jones never attempted to kill David Frost. Eventually, he turned the phone messages and other evidence over to the police. The St. Louis Blues, having lost the first two games of the series against San Jose, won Game 3 at home. And in a very tight and competitive Game 4, Mike Danton scored the only NHL playoff goal of his life. "He played very well in those two games in St. Louis," said Pleau. "He was a good player becoming a better player. He was very valuable to our team, an energy guy. Those kind of guys can really help you. If you have the right kind of energy player, what a difference that can be for your team. He could have been a very valuable player for us, long term."

When the Sharks returned to San Jose for Game 5, Mike Danton seemed as pesky off the ice as on. For whatever reason, he wouldn't take no for an answer from Ronnie Jones, even though Jones had told him his services were not for hire. Danton phoned Jones again, still trying to close the deal that would remove David Frost from his life.

"Hey Ronnie, it's Mike calling. It's around seven o'clock our time. I'm in San Jose now.

"Just wondering what went on last night. Nothing happened. I was just wondering, if you know, what was going on. If you can't, if you can't do this, you know, let me know so I can try and find another way to do this because it's getting real serious. He's [Frost] got another couple people coming down now. He's still at my place tonight and tomorrow night by himself, so I'll try and get a hold of you, man.

"Listen, help me out any way you can, please. It's a matter of life and death for me. All right, I'll try to get in touch with you. Thanks, man. Bye."

Hiring an assassin to kill your agent is a pretty big step in anyone's life. Breaking the law, severing emotional ties, betraying trust—and turning away from the teammates you're supposed to be fighting for—all this marks a point of no return for a young man contemplating murder. And Mike Danton took this step not once but twice.

Ronnie Jones was not the only hit man Danton approached. While that in itself is puzzling, how he chose to go about his clumsy business is stunning.

In the same month that Danton first began negotiating with Ronnie Jones, he became familiar with a young woman named Katie Wolfmeyer. The two met at the Ice Zone, the usual practice rink for the Blues. Wolfmeyer, a nineteen-year-old community college athlete, was working at the rink as a skating instructor for young kids. Wolfmeyer, a groupie of sorts, was clearly infatuated with Danton and while they wouldn't be considered boyfriend and girlfriend, according to Danton, they slept together at least a couple of times before the playoff series with the Sharks. In fact, at Danton's last game in St. Louis, the night he scored his only playoff goal, Katie was there wearing a "We Want Danton" T-shirt. It wouldn't be long before the FBI in St. Louis might have been wearing similar garb.

Prior to Game 5, Danton called Katie from San Jose and told her a story. He said that someone was coming from Canada to kill him in St. Louis. He told her he needed help. He needed to find someone to "take care" of this person. He asked her if she knew anyone who could.

As preposterous as it may appear, with seemingly no one else to turn to, Danton called a teenaged college volleyball player, a gushing young student of no real experience, and asked her if she could find someone to murder his agent. Even for Danton, that was an unusual and amateurish step.

As a partner in crime, Wolfmeyer wasn't an inspired choice. The night she heard from Danton, Wolfmeyer met a police dispatcher named Justin Levi Jones in a bar. (Danton seemed to have bad luck with guys named Jones.) The two began to talk. They had known each other less than an hour before she was on the phone with Danton, proposing her new friend as a candidate for the job of killing Frost. Danton, incredibly, gave Wolfmeyer the go-ahead to negotiate a hit with a guy she'd just met.

"She said that she had a friend that needed a favour," Levi Jones told Bob McKeown of *the fifth estate* in an interview. "So I asked her to elaborate, you know, see what was going on. And she said that Mike was having problems with someone. And, you know, we kept hitting here and hitting there and finally she just said that he had a favour that he wanted done and she wanted to talk ... he wanted to talk with me because she told him about me."

Levi Jones also provided McKeown with a shocking testimonial regarding Danton's confused state of mind at the time. McKeown asked Levi Jones if Danton knew he worked for the police.

"Yes he did," was the answer.

"She's known you less than an hour and he puts this to you, though he knows you work for the police department?" McKeown asked in an interview that didn't appear on television.

"Yes, because she [Katie] told him that before she handed the phone to me and he must have, he just believed everything. He was just like, 'You're not going to tell on me, are you?' You know, he said stuff like that."

On the phone with Danton, Levi Jones wanted to know what he was being asked to do. "I had to ask him numerous times in numerous different ways what it was that he wanted done, because he didn't want to come out and say it directly. And he was secretive and whispering on the phone. He was just very strange to talk to. And eventually I said, 'Like taken care of? You want him beaten up?' And he said, no, like taken care of permanently."

They even talked about a price: $10,000, with the first $3,000 to be made available in his apartment safe, which would be left unlocked. He could first take the $3,000, wrapped individually in $1,000 packets, and the rest would come later on.

"His exact words were, 'It's a matter of life and death' and that he's desperate," said Levi Jones. "And he said that he was begging."

The next morning, Levi Jones went to his Columbia police office and began the work that would send Mike Danton to prison. He would wear a police wire that night, act the part of hit man, carry a gun (although not loaded), and look as though he was attempting to murder Frost.

As muddled as the attempts may have seemed, it was very clear where the police were headed: Levi Jones was fully prepared to act the part of the assassin, right to the point of not pulling the trigger, to implicate Katie Wolfmeyer in a federal crime that had already crossed state lines because of the long-distance calls made and to have Danton arrested for his part in attempting to arrange a murder.

Levi Jones picked up Katie Wolfmeyer at her home, drove to the address Danton had provided, and began the sting operation. But they were first stopped by the security guard at Danton's apartment complex. The guard asked who they were there to see and then requested some identification. He let Levi Jones and Wolfmeyer in through the secured gates and buzzed up to Danton's apartment to let whoever was there know that someone was visiting.

As Levi Jones looked for a parking spot, and Wolfmeyer issued directions, a man appeared on Danton's apartment balcony.

"He was rather a large man, kind of scruffy looking," said Levi Jones. "He was walking quickly toward the vehicle. So I backed up and tried to maintain distance and started back down toward the gate and heading out. And when I got down to the bottom, the security guard stopped me. And he asked me again who I was there to see and what I was doing there. And this man, who was coming toward me, was up on the next level on the balcony looking down and asking the same thing, yelling out you know, 'Who are you here to see? What do you want?'"

The man yelling was David Frost.

When Frost heard who Levi Jones was there to see, he snapped, "Well, I'm Mike Danton." And when Levi Jones said, "No, you're not," Frost replied, "Well, I'm Mike's father."

"I was trying to get away from them, trying to get out. And the security guard was, he was kind of clueless," said Levi Jones. "He was trying to figure out what was going on and he was looking at the man looking at me. I told him I'd be back and I left."

The plot that Danton had scripted as crime drama had descended into farce. The police informant, whom Danton and Wolfmeyer thought was a hit man, was running from Frost, who he thought might be Steve Jefferson. There were so many lies and misunderstandings in play that in the chaotic moment, the fake killer was running from the fake victim.

Levi Jones parked not far from Danton's apartment complex at an arranged location and waited for the police to arrive.

"So we're sitting there for maybe five minutes, you know eight minutes, something like that. And she's just, you know, totally nervous about the whole thing and I think I was telling her that I was going back in there and I was going to take care of it. She said no, just wait for Mike to call. She wanted to talk to him and see what he thought about this and who that was in his apartment. Everybody had questions, you know. She didn't even know what was going on at that point—who the man was and what was going on."

Levi Jones let the nervous Wolfmeyer continue talking while he waited for police. But she was unaware of that. He told her he was going back in to finish the job as soon as possible. He said little in the vehicle as they waited.

"I wanted to know what she knew and I didn't know who this guy was [outside the apartment]," said Levi Jones. "It was either … she said he kind of looked like his agent and this man's saying it's his dad. I'm thinking that she knows more than she's telling me. So I'm saying oh, he wanted us to kill his dad? You know I'm saying it like I can't believe he wanted us to kill his dad. And she kept, she was just in her own world. She's saying that kind of looked like his agent, I've never seen his dad, I don't think his dad would stay at his house. You know, just a number of things. And about the time that she stops talking, she gets quiet for a minute."

In that minute, David Frost's spontaneous lie crystallized into a half-truth that would linger over the Frost–Danton case for years. Because Wolfmeyer and the police informant were confused enough by Frost's dissimulation that they retreated, that confusion still persists. But there is another curious dimension to Frost's claim that he was Steve Jefferson—if Jones really had been a hit man, that lie would have saved Frost's life.

As Wolfmeyer sat in baffled silence, police cars began to surround Levi Jones's vehicle. Minutes later, the young woman was in custody, sobbing.

Levi Jones was sitting in a police vehicle when his cellphone rang again. It was Danton calling from San Jose. The bizarre loop had taken only minutes to close. Immediately after encountering a man hired to kill him, Frost was on the phone with the guy who had sent him. The weird chain of events was both confusing and simplistic.

Danton had called Levi Jones to finalize the hit. Levi Jones had apparently been arrested for what was to have been an attempt on Frost's life. Almost immediately upon the arrest, the FBI arrived to talk to Frost. Quickly, Frost called Danton.

And afterwards, Danton called Levi Jones again. "He was frantic, totally panicked. He said to tell the police that I didn't know him and that Katie and I were over there because she wanted to go see me. And he just babbled on and finally he had to get off the phone again."

When the police began to question David Frost, he first identified himself as Steve Jefferson, Mike Danton's father. The cops knew better. They had been informed of the details prior to the sting. The police on the scene did notice that the safe in Danton's apartment was left open, with $3,000 neatly wrapped in three envelopes.

The night Katie Wolfmeyer was taken into custody by St. Louis police, the Blues were eliminated from the NHL playoffs. It was April 15, 2004. While the impressionable young woman was behind bars, no doubt wondering how things had gone so wrong, the Blues players were returning to their San Jose hotel for the night. Their season had ended in defeat, but the prospect of the long summer months ahead with family and friends at the cottage or the golf course probably took some of the sting out of their disappointment. Not so for Mike Danton, however. Danton did not go to sleep, and didn't have a summer vacation with loved ones on his mind. Instead, he abandoned his teammates, and made his way to the San Jose International Airport hours before the guys he'd flown in with the day before. Then he did something uncharacteristic for professional hockey players. He booked his own flight home on United Airlines, with a connection through Denver.

"We didn't know he had left the team," said Larry Pleau. "We didn't know anything. We found out when everybody else found out. And we were completely stunned."

Earlier that night, his roommate Ryan Johnson told police, Danton had been texting Frost from the Blues' dressing room between periods. By that point, the murder he thought he'd contracted had not taken place. Danton was a wreck. Johnson told police that Danton was weeping in the dressing room.

Before getting on his plane, a confused and nervous Danton called Wolfmeyer again and left messages on her cellphone. His habitual state of confusion and distraction was clearly inflamed. His hockey team had lost that night. His best NHL season was over. And the murder he had somehow found the focus to try to arrange had fallen apart badly. He was on the run.

"Listen, this is what you have to say if anybody talks to you," Danton told Wolfmeyer. "I already talked to Justin. Just say that I've never talked to Justin before, you know, I don't know him. Say that he's a friend of yours and that he came with you to my house because you wanted to see me. You wanted to talk to me and ask what's going on ... because remember I told you I don't want any unexpected visitors.

"So what you have to say to the police, if they call you, be calm. Listen, there's nothing that's going to happen because you guys did nothing wrong. All you have to say is, listen, you know, I was with Mike twice, you know. I saw him twice, and you tell them we had sex or whatever and just say I know that he didn't want me to come to the house unexpectedly. So I brought one of my friends and I just wanted him to knock on the door and talk to Mike, and you know, just let me know that I was here and if it is okay that we could talk. And that's it.

"I don't know Justin and he doesn't know me. We've never talked before.... Once you get this message, erase it. Okay? Bye. I'll talk to you soon."

And then he called back, just a few minutes later.

"Also, Katie, one more thing. If I call you again on the phone, pretend that I haven't talked to you in over a month. If I talk to you about Justin, because they might want me to call you, and see if we have coerced [him]. So just pretend that I haven't talked to you in a long time and I've never talked to Justin. Okay?

"Try and do that. Once you get these messages, erase them. Okay? Bye-bye. Be strong for us. This'll work out. I know it will."

Mike Danton left for the airport in San Jose intent on making it back to St. Louis, though what he hoped to accomplish there was unclear. But he never made his flight. He was arrested by the FBI holding a boarding pass, and charged with conspiring to commit murder, the charges being even more serious because the telephone calls crossed state lines. Young Katie Wolfmeyer faced similar charges in the murder-for-hire plot, but she was acquitted by a jury five months later.

Danton was not nearly so fortunate. At the age of 23, just after establishing himself as a hockey player of value, after dedicating so much of his life to getting there, Mike Danton's professional hockey career ended in handcuffs. His next uniform would be that of the Santa Clara County Department of Corrections, the fifth largest prison in California. He would never play another game in the National Hockey League.

The question is *why?*

Why did Danton's promising career have to come to such a senseless end? What happened to cause the most focused of young hockey players to lose that focus and his freedom along with it? Why did Danton want Frost dead so urgently, smack in the middle of his first foray in the Stanley Cup playoffs? Why did he want his agent, supposedly his surrogate father, murdered?

Sometimes, when we ask questions, we don't really expect a simple answer. But in this case, there may be an answer, or at least part of one. And if not an answer, then certainly a thread of troubling connections.

This story is tied up in the game of hockey, the culture that surrounds the sport, and the intensity of the intertwined relationships between coach, player, and family. It's even more entangled when you consider the difficult family history and a series of troubling and disastrous decisions. By the time he found himself behind prison bars, more than half of Mike Danton's life had been spent under the wing of David Frost. To understand how he got there means going back to the moment their paths first crossed.

2

Young Mike and Minor-Hockey Life

On the drive home from a summer hockey league game, after scoring six goals, Mike Jefferson announced, "Dad, I'm going to play in the NHL."

He was six years old at the time, playing hockey in his first organized league, and it was the kind of proclamation any young boy might make. But Mike Jefferson wasn't just any young boy, and when his father heard the words, he stored them away proudly in the back of his mind.

There was, he thought, something different about his son when compared to the other kids. Mike had, from the beginning, this fire within him, and an inherent passion for hockey. He loved the game as much as his father was obsessed with it. His father says proudly that his son was born full of "piss and vinegar." It wasn't the talent Steve Jefferson noticed. It was his drive to succeed.

Steve won't forget that six-goal game, or his son's words. "You hear something like that, you don't forget about it."

And he remembers that day for another reason: In order for him to be at the game, he had to miss out on a business opportunity. "I went to the game because I always went to the game," said Steve Jefferson. "I was supposed to be somewhere else. I lost a big account because of it. I lost Sun Pac Juices that day...."

That became part of the trade-off: hockey vs. business. Mike's hockey, in Steve's mind, came first. Mike came first. Then there was everything else.

Mike Jefferson was one of those kids who was just born to play. He had it in him. He wore NHL pyjamas, demanded there be NHL wallpaper on his walls, NHL pillow slips on his bed, and almost everything he did or talked about had a hockey twist to it. He would skate all day on the backyard rink and come inside only for meals. Half the time, he didn't even realize he'd frozen his feet until he came indoors, got his skates off, and his toes began to thaw and throb. But he didn't care. He would do it day after winter's day, by himself, with friends, with his father.

"He was a rambunctious kid, full of life," said his mom, Sue. "But he was a good kid. There was a little hellion in him. He was non-stop, full of activity, but he was full of energy and fun. He was always going. He exhausted us at times. And he was hard to keep up with."

He was also athletic in a way neither of his parents were. Steve had been a middle-of-the-road hockey player as a kid, more interested in girls and partying. Sue was more the athletic one. She was a gymnast and a swimmer and a ballet dancer of enough quality to appear in *Swan Lake* at Maple Leaf Gardens. That was her performance highlight.

But neither had the non-stop drive that was inside their firstborn son. At the age of eleven, Mike heard about a hockey-playing buddy who ran mini-triathlons in the summer. His friend was among the best in the province. And without any kind of training or preparation, Mike decided to give it a shot. As things turned out, not only did he finish it, but he also beat his provincially ranked friend and won the triathlon—and was invited to compete at the next level. That's the kind of athlete Mike Jefferson was. He never did run another triathlon, retiring undefeated. He just did that one for fun and was being recruited to the next level immediately.

It wasn't very different for him in hockey. Most kids begin in house league and advance from there. But Mike went straight from a learn-to-play program to summer league to higher-level "rep" hockey with the Chinguacousy Blues without really missing a beat, his first competitive team at the young age of seven. It was while playing for Chinguacousy that he began his lifelong friendship with Sheldon Keefe. And Steve Jefferson found a best friend himself in Sheldon's father, Brian Keefe.

Life couldn't have been better for a young hockey player and his ambitious father. The Keefes and the Jeffersons did everything together. They were on the move in the very competitive world of kids' hockey. Sheldon was the best player on the Blues. Mike was the second best player.

"Sheldon always had more skill than Mike, and Mike was the more physical player of the two," said Steve. "As the years went on, Sheldon would depend more and more on Mike to do the dirty stuff for him while he took care of the finesse.

"I think back to those days and I think everything seemed so pure from a hockey standpoint. How could anything have gone so wrong?"

Everything was all about hockey for young Mike. But his focus sharpened about the time he discovered a favourite team and a favourite player. Mike was born in 1980. Steve Yzerman was drafted into the NHL in 1983. And very quickly, everything

Jefferson aspired to be was about the great captain, Yzerman. Mike became fixated on everything Yzerman, everything hockey.

He had to have an Yzerman jersey. His parents were soon peeling off the NHL wallpaper to paint the walls Detroit Red Wings red and white.

"He actually started out as a Leaf fan," said Steve Jefferson. "But when Yzerman started going good, it became all about him. Not just for him, but for his brother, too. With the two boys, it was Yzerman this, Yzerman that. Guess they couldn't have picked a better guy to follow."

The Chinguacousy Blues, led by Keefe and Jefferson, were just an average team at the very competitive AAA level of rep hockey. Eventually, both would grow to be too big and too talented to remain on a middle-of-the-road minor-hockey team. The competition is too fierce when it comes to recruiting talent in youth hockey. It would be only a matter of time before both would move on and up. But not without incident first from Steve Jefferson.

At the atom level of hockey, which includes ten-year-old players, Chinguacousy made it all the way to the finals of an out-of-town tournament in Barrie, beating the famous and favoured Toronto Marlies 5–4 in an upset victory to get there. By the standards of minor hockey, that victory was about as good as it gets. Sheldon scored four goals and one assist in the game. Mike had one goal and four assists. That night, at the tournament dance in a local hotel, the Chinguacousy coach took Steve Jefferson aside on the dance floor and told him he was going to start the backup goalie in the championship game the following day. Jefferson was not impressed.

"I kind of lost it with him," said Steve. "I said to him, 'This is rep hockey. It's costing us 500–600 bucks to be here for the weekend. You have to play your best goalie. You can't use that other kid.'"

Just as he turned on the dance floor after arguing with the coach, the father of the backup goalie, having overheard the conversation, took a swing at him. "He was mad," said Steve. "He overheard what I was saying to the coach. I didn't back down. I was just saying, 'I don't care if they play your kid the next three games—it's not fair to the other kids to play him tomorrow and it's not fair to us.' You have to play your best players. That's what rep hockey is. You have to make rep decisions."

The next day, with the backup goalie in net, Chinguacousy was blown out in the championship final.

"After that game, I told the coach, this will be our last season here. I said to him, 'Lose my number.' I'd had it with him and the way he coached. And after that, we got involved in the whole recruiting thing with AAA hockey. If you're not in it, it's hard to explain what it's all about. It can be pretty cruel and consuming if you don't know what's going on. There's all kinds of game playing going on. People are promising you this, people promising you that. All kinds of lies being told. Come here and we'll give you this. Play here and we'll give you that.

"If you don't know how it works, minor hockey at the AAA level can be a very nasty place and it can eat you up. And even if you do know how it works, it can be just as nasty."

The higher the level Mike Jefferson played, the more intense he became about hockey. "He was very hard on himself," said his mom, Sue. "If he made a mistake, if he did something wrong, if he lost a game, he took it very hard. That was something inside of him that wasn't necessarily inside of us. He was not very forgiving of mistakes that he made. No matter what he did, he always thought he should do better."

Steve Jefferson can't forget the drives to the rink. On the highway, making their way from Brampton to midtown Toronto, Mike Jefferson would climb from the back seat into the front, turn off the music in the van, and say, "Okay, Dad, get me going."

Rolling through the Canadian winter, the son would badger the father for more coaching, more inspiration.

"Start working me," Mike would say. "Tell me everything I've got to do."

"And we'd go through things. What he needed to do on every shift. How hard he had to play. How he had to finish his checks. How he had to play in the defensive zone. Just details about the game. He wanted to hear everything. It got him all pumped up to play. We had this relationship and all of it centred on hockey."

Even at home, it was all about hockey. "He'd sit on my lap and we'd watch hockey every night of the week on television. Sue would come in the room and say it's time for bed, it's nine o'clock, and I'd convince her it was okay for him to stay up and watch hockey with me."

A lot of nights, Mike Jefferson would fall asleep in his father's lap watching hockey. It was dad and son and hockey. That was their life.

From the small-town games of the Chinguacousy Blues, Mike Jefferson advanced to what was then known as the Metropolitan Toronto Hockey League, the largest and most competitive minor-hockey league in Canada (the former MTHL is now called the Greater Toronto Hockey League). Mike would join the Toronto Red Wings, coached by Brian Passmore and his assistant coach, Bob Goodenow, who was on his way to becoming arguably the most powerful man in hockey as executive director of the NHL Players' Association.

The tryout process for most minor-hockey teams in the Toronto area is something of a sham. It's not about tryouts as much as it is about coronations. Most coaches don't pick their players at tryout—the process is too difficult and too arduous for that. They pick their players before tryouts. They scout, recruit, promise the moon, and carefully select the right people for the right positions. Mike Jefferson was one of the chosen ones in his early years. He was a player in demand.

At the time, residency rules determined who could play where in minor hockey in Toronto. Where you lived had a bearing on where you could play. Jefferson was recruited by the Toronto Marlies, the team Chinguacousy had beaten in Barrie, but that didn't turn out well. They eventually passed on him—in an illegal pre-tryout tryout—reneging on promises they'd made to Steve. Passmore, the Red Wings coach, approached the coach of the powerful Brampton team and asked him a simple question: "If Jefferson lived on the other side of Dixie Road [the residency border], would he make your team?" The coach said *definitely*. Right then, Passmore committed to having Jefferson play for his Red Wings. "We were very excited," said Steve Jefferson. "We didn't realize then there was a pecking order on the team and that we weren't part of it."

Being part of a new team on the rise is always an exciting proposition. There is a certain status in the sport attached to being on the right team at the right time. The competition is beyond fierce. The excitement of being one of the chosen ones is extreme. Every young hockey player with ambition—in tandem with every young hockey player's ambitious parents—wants to be on the best AAA team. Getting there is the first step. Staying there can often be even more challenging.

It isn't always about talent or ability. It can often be about cold economics. The more resources a family has, the more money it can bring to a team in donation or sponsorship, the better chance the young player has of first making it, then getting additional playing time. This was a lesson the Jeffersons learned very early in their AAA experience.

"That was a money team and we didn't have a lot of money." The budget to operate high-end AAA hockey teams can often be astronomical. Many will exceed $100,000 for a season, which will include year-round practices, extra tournaments, extra ice, and extra instruction. Being able to access money, either your own or via sponsorship, can make a difference for a player and a family.

"If you pumped a lot of money into the team, you got special favours, like more ice time during games [for your child]," said Steve Jefferson. "A lot of minor-hockey teams operate that way. It's not how good a player you are; it's who do you know and how much money are you willing to put into the team? Passmore was the coach, so his kid played a ton and Goodenow was the assistant coach, so his kid played a ton. And the money guys played. Mike turned out better than all those kids and he barely got to play. And there wasn't anything I could do about it.

"After some games with the Red Wings, Mike would come home crying. 'Why aren't I playing more? Why are they benching me so much?' I didn't really have a good answer to give him. Passmore wasn't giving him the opportunity. I wasn't going to tell Mike it was because we didn't have enough money. Years later, when he got to junior hockey, I think Mike took some pleasure in beating up Passmore's kid a couple of times in games. That was like some kind of payback for him."

In the summer, AAA hockey teams often form off-season all-star teams of sorts. It keeps the kids on the ice, training year round, forever striving to make it bigger in hockey. The competition is intense. The payoff at the end is that minor-hockey players begin to build reputations. At each age group, the best of the best are quickly identified and followed closely. Jefferson was one of those players.

The Red Wings put together a summer-league team and one of their real competitors was a team called the Brampton All-Stars. Brampton had a very strong group of players from the 1980 birth year, many of whom would become known later on. But none would be as well known as the coach of the team, a man Steve Jefferson recognized from seeing him around in the rinks, hearing about him, and knowing about his hockey school.

The year was 1990. The coach's name: David Frost.

3

Frost Warnings

Just who is David Frost and how is it he came to be the central figure in so many shattered lives?

That remains a question without easy answers, more than ten years after his name became known around Canada and in hockey circles for all the wrong reasons. Frost has been kicked out of nearly every league he's been associated with. He has been investigated by the Ontario Provincial Police not once but three times, and by the Peel Regional Fire Department for suspected arson. Curiously for a man who is best known for being the intended victim of a murder plot, Frost has even been accused of hiring muscle to settle scores of his own.

He has been described by his many detractors as evil; as a clown and cruel manipulator of vulnerable young people; as cunning, nurturing, controlling, ambitious, and paranoid. Or, as columnist Rosie DiManno once wrote in the *Toronto Star*, "[He's] a creep and a bully and a repugnant human being. But there's no law against that."

From the beginning, coming out of Bramalea Secondary School, Frost was something of an outcast. As a teenager, he looked "like a weedy little pencil neck, a bully magnet," wrote Gare Joyce of *espn: the magazine*. As an adult, that changed. With his round and unshaven face, unkempt appearance, slight pot belly and an intentionally intimidating presence, he certainly looked the part of bully. It was a look that worked for him; and along with it, he certainly acted the part.

But one thing about Frost: he knew hockey. That much you had to say about him. The kids who attended his hockey schools improved their skills. The teams he coached, in minor hockey, junior hockey, all levels, were impressive, even if his methods were often in question. He found young players with promise, trained them, developed them—some might say controlled them—but from his small group, the success rate of his development was extraordinarily high. Hockey was what Frost did best: Getting where he wanted to go in life, that was another matter entirely.

It was Frost's intention to become a somebody in the hockey world. Somebody who mattered.

And yet, for all his hockey acumen and insight into the game, Frost seemed to wear out his welcome wherever he coached. No matter where he went or which team he was involved with, trouble somehow followed him. His docket of hockey crimes and misdemeanours, real and imagined, is lengthy and alarming. Hardly a year went by that Frost didn't somehow clash with the authorities of the sport—and yet for a while, he kept bouncing from fresh start to fresh start.

What all his blunders have in common is Frost's habit of resorting to fear and intimidation, and his contempt for the rules. While coaching the Brampton tier-two junior team, he was banned by the Ontario Hockey Association after the 1993 season. That was his first significant coaching job. It probably should have been his last. Getting suspended in hockey isn't all that difficult; getting banned is another matter entirely.

The sixteen- to twenty-year-olds Frost coached had a reputation for fighting during games, after games, before games. The brawls, he once admitted to the *Toronto Sun*, were often orchestrated. It was all about intimidation with Frost. He intimidated his players. They, in turn, intimidated the opposition. It was them against the world, with the young coach believing that through orchestrated violence, he would make a name for himself.

He made a name all right. Not a name most hockey people would be proud of, but a name nonetheless. He was intimidating and so were his teams. The Brampton team, after too many incidents, was put on watch by the OHA—the squad showed a distasteful style of play for what was thought to be a league of development. It wasn't any one incident that found Frost in trouble: It was everything. The attitude of the players. The attitude of the coach. The concern for other teams in the OHA. Finally, the league would take no more. Citing what league president Brent Ladds called the Brampton team's "incredibly undisciplined and unruly play," the OHA placed the entire franchise on probation and brought them back into the fold only once the league was convinced by the ownership of the team that Frost would not return as coach.

"To this day," said Ladds back in 1999, "David Frost is persona non grata in the OHA. If he ever wanted to coach in our league again, he would have to present himself before the board."

Frost never did present himself to the board. But being investigated became a central part of Frost's life.

In 1993, after being kicked out of tier-two junior hockey, Frost returned to coaching, taking a position with the Toronto Young Nationals (or the Young Nats, as they are known). At the time, that was considered a giant step backwards for a coach who thought he was on the move, even though the Nats have long been a prestigious grooming ground for young players, a place where legends such as Mike Gartner, Paul Coffey, and Eric Lindros played as kids.

But even there, Frost managed to botch things. He was suspended indefinitely by the Metropolitan Toronto Hockey League (soon to be the GTHL). In a letter dated September 26, 1996, Frost was informed of his suspension for being party to the "falsification of documents." Allegedly, the signature of Young Nats general manager Terry Weir was forged on the player-release forms, which, in essence, broke up a championship team.

Frost claimed in a lengthy interview with the *Toronto Sun* in 1999 that he didn't forge anyone's name on the player-release forms. "I just wrote my name," he said.

But he was not the signing person of authority to offer releases to the players. Frost has also maintained he filed a lawsuit against the GTHL and its president John Gardner for comments made about him. But the GTHL, to this day, claims that no lawsuit was ever filed and there are no court accounts of Frost's suit being filed.

Frost had been the coach of the Young Nats team for three seasons, guiding young hockey players from the ages of twelve to fifteen, with his success culminating in winning the 1996 Ontario provincial bantam championships. But his plans extended beyond the Young Nats. He wanted to take his chosen players with him to form the kind of championship team he managed in minor hockey, and move them as a group to the next level. The only way to free up the players was to have them released.

Having illegally released all his players from the Toronto Young Nationals, Frost was now free to take his players wherever he could clump them all together. He actually shopped his players around as a group. At first, he found a place for them to play. When the 1996 hockey season began, Frost's illegally released chosen players wound up playing for the Bramalea Blues of the Ontario Provincial Junior Hockey League—another league Frost was, in fact, banned from. But the Bramalea experience didn't last long.

As it turned out, Frost's time away from coaching lasted all of eight games. And this time, Frost didn't have to forge any documents to bring his players with him. He just picked up his boys and skipped town—leaving the Bramalea team in total disarray. And having essentially been banned from two enormous and powerful leagues in just three short years, it was not surprising that Frost's next step as a coach came in what is known as an outlaw league: the now-defunct Metro Junior Hockey League. Early that season, Frost wound up taking all five of the players out of the Greater Toronto Area to the outlaw MJHL, the only league that would accept players without releases. They went to a small town in Ontario called Deseronto and suited up for a first-year (and what turned out to be a last-year) team called the Quinte Hawks. Officially, Frost was the assistant coach when he arrived midway through the season. Unofficially, though, he ran the team on the ice and off the ice, and kept remarkably close tabs on his boys while living in the now-infamous Bay View Inn, in a modest suite with three of his players.

An outlaw league gets its name when it operates outside the rules of Hockey Canada and the provincial governing organizations. Those types of leagues are set up to be answerable to no one: They make their own rules. They honour no signed contracts or agreements from other leagues, and often outlaw leagues are set up to give hungry parents who believe their hockey-playing child is missing out on mainstream development another supposed legitimate shot at junior hockey. The more junior teams, the more junior leagues, the more parents believe their child is the next star. These are the hockey schools of harder knocks. Major junior hockey may be the Harvard of hockey for developing players and parents who clasp onto the dream. The outlaw league is the college at the corner in the strip mall that may not be there next week.

Even someone with no knowledge of hockey would spot the difference between the glitzy world of AAA hockey in Toronto and the gritty reality of the MJHL. The old six hundred–seat rink where the Hawks played, Deseronto Arena, didn't have glass behind the nets, as most rinks do. Fans coped with steel mesh instead, leading to an inevitable nickname for the arena: the Chicken Coop.

The Hawks started their inaugural season with a woeful 1–5 record. But if that was a problem, the solution may have been worse. To turn the team around, the Hawks brought in David Frost. If there was one thing Frost knew how to do, it was to win through intimidation. And soon enough, other teams started coming down with the "Deseronto flu": a mysterious ailment that kept players out of the lineup when their teams were visiting the Chicken Coop.

The police were called to Quinte Hawks games five times that season, the first time less than two weeks after Frost arrived. There were incidents of fans throwing bottles, of Frost wielding fire extinguishers against opposing players in a brawl in the hallway between the dressing rooms, of Hawks players swinging sticks. One night, when the Pickering Panthers were in town, the Hawks' goon provoked a brawl during the warm-up, before the referees were even on the ice, and the home side enjoyed open season on the hapless visitors. When the sticks and gloves had been cleared off the ice, and the game finally began, the Hawks pummelled the Panthers again, winning the game 7–3.

That's how Frost's Hawks won. The team went on an eleven-game winning streak when Frost took over.

Frost and the kids he'd brought with him from the Young Nats were the talk of the very small town. It was Frost's greatest season—four of his tier-two junior players would go on to play in the NHL—yet it was the undoing of whatever decent reputation he had. The first-year team was flourishing. The new young hockey players had everybody talking. Small towns and hockey teams can meld that way. This started out as a love affair of a hockey season but things didn't end that way.

Some coaches are known for being strict disciplinarians and for challenging their players. But fans at the Deseronto Arena could hardly believe what they saw on the Hawks bench during a playoff game. Frost turned and first berated one of his players, then slugged him in the jaw. It wasn't just any punch. It was the knockout punch for his coaching career. The player was Darryl Tiveron, who lived with Frost at the Bay View Inn, who had worked at his hockey school in Brampton, and who would later work for him again. He was one of Frost's boys—one of the loyal kids in this tight-knit group. But the punch wasn't a hidden moment of any kind. It was seen by everybody in the building. It quickly became the talk of the town. In fact, off-duty police officers in the crowd witnessed the punch and were ready to lay charges right there.

Frost was, in fact, charged and later pleaded guilty to misdemeanour assault charges, even though every member of his team was prepared to testify under oath that the punch seen by an entire arena crowd had never occurred. That, as much as anything, spoke of the climate of control and fear in which Frost operated his teams. An entire team was willing to lie to police for their coach.

"I had two choices," Frost said in his 1999 interview with the

Toronto Sun. "I could have gone to court and won, or I plead guilty and prevent all the kids on my team from having to go to court and testify. My lawyer went into chambers and came out and said, 'You plead guilty to grabbing and pointing at him, you pay $250, and you'll have no criminal record.' I decided to plead guilty, but I refuse to allow anyone to say I punched this kid when I did not." Amazingly, having just pleaded guilty to abusing a player in his charge, Frost managed to depict himself as the defender of his players.

But even the outlaw MJHL wasn't buying the act, and Frost found himself suspended once again. As soon as he left the Hawks' bench, the word was, the Brampton players he had brought in basically shut their games down in protest for the rest of the season. Quinte was eliminated early in the playoffs. The Tiveron game was the last time David Frost ever coached a hockey team.

In his interview with the *Sun*, Frost defended his many actions and accusations. "I don't care what the outside perception of me is. I don't care what others think. I don't care who I piss off or who I step on. I don't believe in kissing ass. I didn't come into this business to make friends.

"I've heard the brainwash stuff, that I brainwash players. Maybe I have brainwashed them. You know how crazy that is. If I was that smart, I would brainwash twenty of them and we would go win the Stanley Cup. Brainwashing? When I hear that cult stuff, it makes me crazy.

"I've heard it said I'm controlling these kids. But I won't apologize for it. If having too much influence means my players go to school, they maintain 75-plus averages, they work hard in games, they don't stay out at night, they never break curfew—if that means too much influence, then I'm guilty.

"Success breeds jealousy," he boasted. "I kind of like the controversy, as long as I know what I'm doing is best for the player. I don't care who I rub the wrong way. I'm not about to change. Not for anybody."

Exactly what kind of success Frost believed had provoked this envy is not clear. He had been, in order, permanently kicked out of the OHA, indefinitely suspended from the MTHL, and suspended from the Metro Junior League. All within four seasons. Envy should have been the least of his worries.

Until that season with the Hawks, the problems with Frost were all hockey-related. It was in Deseronto that the seedy legend of Frost began to take shape.

The stories of the questionable behaviour of Frost and his tight group of hockey players have been told in many forms over the years and led later to widespread sexual exploitation charges against Frost, which he had to face in a Napanee, Ontario, courtroom in 2008. Accounts of two-fisted drinking, partying, and three-way sex in Room 22 of the Bay View Inn have figured prominently in newspaper coverage, television documentaries and, of course, trial testimony. One of the first people to raise concerns about Frost was the Hawks' trainer, Chuck Morgan. He didn't like Frost or his methods, and Morgan was troubled by things he saw. These were still young boys in his mind. What were they doing with Frost?

"I was uncomfortable with a lot of the things that went on," said Morgan. "We'd be on the bus, travelling from a game, and Dave would call up [a player] from the back of the bus to come give him a massage. This wasn't just any massage. [The player] would be wearing his underwear and nothing else. And I don't know about you, but it didn't look right to me to have a sixteen-year-old boy standing only in his underwear, rubbing his coach. It made me very uncomfortable.

"I don't know a lot of sixteen-year-old boys who would want to do that in front of everybody. It was like he commanded something, and they did it. That's the way it worked."

But it wasn't his coaching so much as it was Frost's close relationship with his players that created a climate of suspicion and silence around him. This has been an inherent problem with all minor sports, but mostly with hockey. There is a motto used in hockey dressing rooms, where the code of silence rules, that is similar to one used by those who attend Alcoholics Anonymous meetings:

> *What you see here*
> *What you say here*
> *When you leave here*
> *Let it stay here*

In other words, what happens in a dressing room, with a team, remains with the team members. It is their business, their story. No one sold that or adhered to that notion better than Frost and his players. They weren't a team, they were a small group within their own team. They did what he said, spoke when he told them to, and grew consumed with pleasing their coach.

Even when Frost's players made their way to the Ontario Hockey League, the major junior league in the province, there were all kinds of whispers surrounding them and their conduct. Fingers were pointed but again there were few people willing to say anything about Frost—to speak out—seemingly afraid of attaching their names to any kind of story involving him. No one would challenge Frost and his authority.

There was, for a lot of reasons, a general fear of being involved in any way with Frost, and people were afraid to say anything about him. One time, a journeyman OHL player named Richard Scott had been in a fight in a game with one of Frost's players. The next time he saw Frost was in the Oshawa Civic Centre and Scott was not dressed for the game, having been serving a suspension. While Scott was standing in the arena, Frost approached him with two large men, attempting to intimidate the on-ice fighter. The message was clear: You touch one of my boys again, we'll touch you. This was no idle threat.

"You should have seen his face when he came back to the dressing room. He was white as a ghost. There was fear in his eyes," said John Goodwin, Scott's coach with the Oshawa Generals. "He came and told us what happened. We didn't know what to say or what to do. All you had to do was take one good look at this kid to know he had been threatened and he was scared to death about it."

The tenor of Frost was threatening to those outside his little world. He had a way of getting what he wanted, when he wanted it, and, for a time, no one in the small world of junior hockey was willing to stop him. And no one, it seemed, was willing to push hard enough to find out what he was capable of.

Just as Frost had manipulated the transfer of his boys from the Young Nats to Bramalea to Quinte, he later manipulated a series of trades in the Ontario Hockey League that led to his boys, four of them, playing for the Toronto St. Michael's Majors franchise. It is, at first glance, surprising that a guy who couldn't hold down a job as a minor-hockey coach could pull strings at the OHL level, but Frost was nothing if not dogged. And his ability to both annoy and manipulate and his innate aggressiveness was helping him get his name noticed—a name he tried to spread around, since he had his sights set on a job in the OHL.

If there was a coaching job opening in junior hockey, he would start a rumour that he was a candidate for the position. In 1998, the Mississauga Ice Dogs, partially owned by Don Cherry, were searching for a coach to turn around that troubled junior team. Frost not only started a rumour that he was a candidate for the coaching job, but also told some media people that he had been interviewed by Cherry for the position.

When Cherry was asked about it, he said he didn't know who Frost was. "Unless he's someone I've shaken hands with, I don't know him. I know he was telling people I interviewed him. But I don't know the guy at all. I wouldn't know him if I fell over him."

Meanwhile, even if Frost wasn't making much progress establishing a career in the OHL, his players were. One kid in particular showed early signs he might be a franchise player for the Sarnia Sting, scoring six goals in his first twelve games as a sixteen-year-old. Those are excellent numbers for such a young player. But if this kid was the future in Sarnia, the future didn't last very long.

This Frost protegé had been billeted with a Sarnia bank manager named Bonnie Gardner. Not long into his stay at her home, Gardner expressed concern to the team about the amount of time Frost was spending at her house, in the player's bedroom. The Sting, which had had its fill of Frost after only a few games, passed that concern on to OHL commissioner David Branch.

"There was concern about the length of time [a player] and Frost spent behind closed doors," said Branch. "We looked into it. We had to get an independent person to investigate the situation. We got some professional advice on this before doing anything.

You have to remember the times. This wasn't a normal happening. And this was all uncharted waters we were in after the Graham James [sexual abuse] situation. Our immediate concern was that this was a case of sexual abuse.

"We wanted to know, 'What's going on here?' But when we looked into it, there was denial all around. It may not have seemed proper, but we didn't really know what it was, other than unusual."

Whatever was determined in the investigation, it was enough for the kid to leave Sarnia prior to being traded to Toronto and general manager Mark Hunter was happy to see him go.

"To me," said Bonnie Gardner, "Frost's a scary person. I don't like him. I get a bad feeling about him. I'm not afraid of him like a lot of people are. I've been doing this for a lot of years [billeting] and I've never seen a situation like that before."

Gardner said those things in 1999, long before Frost was known to the public.

"The guy is a lunatic," Rob Ciccarelli, owner of the Sting and brother of NHL Hall of Famer Dino Ciccarelli, said of Frost and his association with him. "What worried me is he had a cult-like attraction for the player. I have never in my history seen anything like that. The kid totally did everything that Frost said. It was shocking. It got to a point where [the player] would look up during games and take hand signals from Frost. During games, he was always looking up to the stands. It became a terrible situation. We didn't want to trade him but we decided the best thing to do was part company."

That promising young player who spent too much time in his bedroom with David Frost was Mike Jefferson. He was one of the kids released illegally from the Young Nats. He was one of the players who went to the Bramalea Blues, and then followed Frost to the Quinte Hawks. The underwear-clad kid who was forced to give Frost massages on the team bus? Jefferson again.

"I believe he had a plan," said Gord Smith, a police officer in Brampton who was very involved as a minor-hockey coach northwest of Toronto. "I don't know if it started out as a plan, but it sure looks like it did. He targeted low-income kids from Brampton. Kids with hockey talent but not necessarily financial means. Kids from troubled or problematic homes. He brought those kids together when they were pretty young and he made them his. He promised them things. I don't know exactly how he did it, but they became his, and when they became his, he turned almost all of them against their parents.

"I don't know if there's ever been a situation like this before. I'm not sure there will ever be another one again. A lot of people in hockey knew what was going on, or thought they knew what was going on, but nobody said anything. That was the thing with Frost. Nobody ever said anything or challenged it. And nobody was willing to do anything. A lot of the parents, they were all caught up in chasing the dream. They were too blind to see what was going on. I like the Jeffersons, but I think they were one of those families that turned a blind eye to everything.

"Hockey was everything and they couldn't see beyond that.

"And look what happened to them."

If Frost had a favourite player in his stable of Brampton kids, one whom he later would describe as his son, it was the young Mike Jefferson. They met when Jefferson was ten years old and by eleven, Jefferson was playing for Frost both in winter and in summer and attending Frost's Elite Hockey School, where he would later work. There was something about Jefferson that appealed to Frost. Maybe it was his lack of size—he wasn't much taller than five foot seven as a junior. Maybe it was his overt passion to play. Maybe it was a burning desire to succeed, no matter the price involved. Whatever it was, Jefferson, like Frost, was always an underdog. An against-all-odds type of kid. Just like Frost, the high-school outcast.

Jefferson had talent and drive. Frost had the brains. He always had a plot. Behind the bench or in the stands, he could always read the play, always plan ahead. And long before Frost would go on trial himself in 2008, he ushered Mike Jefferson into the Peel Regional Police Department, where Jefferson filed a complaint against his father. In that interview with Detective Chris Benson, Mike alleged that there was verbal abuse in his home and drug problems. He did not allege he had been physically beaten. At the end of the interview, the police officer taking his statement startled Mike Jefferson by announcing he would proceed on the information he had just received. And, he told Jefferson, if it wasn't true, then he would be in some kind of trouble.

"At the end of it, the kid said, 'I don't want the police to do anything about this. I just want this on the record,'" a Peel police officer later said, requesting anonymity. "That kind of threw up alarm bells for us. Why come in and file a complaint and then ask us not to proceed on it? It didn't make sense to any of us at the time. The kid made some accusations that we really couldn't corroborate. Everything he said was unsubstantiated and when we told him we'd like to investigate it, he said no and got pretty upset about it.

"Knowing about Frost, we thought maybe Frost was laying the groundwork for something that would come later. But we didn't know for what. We just thought the whole thing was pretty curious."

4

Tom's Story

At the age of thirteen, Tom Jefferson would often look at photographs of himself with his older brother, Mike. Playing, laughing, doing what kids are supposed to do. But he had no memory of any of those scenes. The people in the photographs looked familiar enough, but the moods, the smiles, and the emotions seemed foreign to him. If there had been good times with his brother, he couldn't recall them. All he knew was that his older brother, the budding pro hockey player, was someone he looked up to, someone he desperately wanted to be like, someone with whom he badly desired a relationship. But he had almost none. Full of a confusing combination of self-confidence and self-doubt, he instinctively knew what was missing from his life. And his parents, from the outside, saw the very same thing.

But while Tom idolized his older brother, Mike seemed to see Tom as no more than an annoyance, and the more Mike got involved in hockey, the less interested he was in his brother and his own family.

"All of a sudden, there came a time in my life where I didn't exist to him," said Tom. "I'd looked up to him big time. I looked up to him as a role model. But even then, I knew we were all being pulled apart. I could sense that.

"Before, I used to go downstairs at home and we'd play Nintendo all the time. Then, once Frost was involved, once Mike was into that whole thing, I'd come downstairs and he'd say things like, 'Get the fuck away from me' or 'You're a little brat.'"

The Jefferson family was broken, though Steve and Sue didn't yet know how badly. They did know what might fix things, however. Tom needed to reach out to Mike. The hope was, maybe, just maybe, doing that would somehow bring the family closer together, and if not, then at least the boys.

So when the invitation came in the summer of 2000 for Tom to spend a week at David Frost's cottage just north of Kingston, it seemed like just what the Jeffersons had been waiting for. Steve and Sue imagined their young son, along with his older brother and his buddies, swimming, boating, and sitting around campfires. It looked like an opportunity for two brothers, seven years apart, to finally bridge the age gap.

"I would look at the pictures and I didn't remember those times," said Tom, an adult at age twenty-four, barely older than Mike was that summer, talking of the photo albums in his home. "They looked like such happy times and everybody was smiling. All I wanted was to feel that. So when I had the opportunity to go to the cottage, to feel like [I did in] those photos, I jumped at it.

"I knew I was a little young and I wondered a little bit, 'Why do they want a thirteen-year-old hanging around them?' The guys were all over twenty or around twenty except Dave. He was a lot older. But I thought, 'It's a cottage. You go fishing, boating. What could go wrong?'"

His mother wasn't convinced at the time. "I didn't want him to go, but he begged us," said Sue Jefferson. "But it was so important for Tom. I'd already lost contact with one son. I didn't want to disappoint the other one. I was worried about what might go on. I was worried about drinking. He was only thirteen. I talked to Larry [Barron, the hockey player] about it, who was living with us around that time. He promised me everything would be okay. I listened to Larry. I trusted Larry. That was a mistake."

Steve Jefferson has a different view: "We wanted to see if he and Mike could bond. Larry Barron said it would be good for them." And as with just about everything else that swirled around the Jefferson household, there was a hockey angle as well. At least, in Steve's mind there was.

"Tom was just as talented a player as Mike was at the same age—just not as into the game the way Mike was," said Steve. "I thought, if Tom can get some of that focus that Mike has, that would help him. That would be good for him. But when he came back from that place, he wasn't the same kid.

"What happened at that cottage stayed with him and has had a terrible effect on his life."

It's a long way from Brampton to David Frost's cottage, which is north of Kingston on Loughborough Lake. But hockey players are used to long drives, and Mike and his buddies, who had been playing major junior for years and had put in a lot of miles on team buses, would have thought nothing of a four-hour jaunt to the lake. But it would not be long before Tom Jefferson was feeling very far from home.

Young guys goof around, and elite hockey players may get a bit rougher than most. But that's not what Tom had to worry about. At first, things seemed normal enough out in the woods. The sun, the water, and more than enough testosterone-fuelled camaraderie to go around in the tight-knit group—for a kid, it was a dream come true. What Tom hadn't taken into account was the cost of joining a group like that. There were, it seems, all kinds of unspoken rules that Tom was about to be "initiated" in, whether he wanted to be or not.

One hot afternoon while the boys were outside, according to Tom, he made his way back to the cool of the cottage and found himself alone in the kitchen. His thoughts turned to ice cream, so he opened the freezer and took a couple of spoonfuls. It was then when Frost spotted him.

"He pretty much lost his fucking mind over this, like I'd stolen something important from him," said Tom. "He said the ice cream is for the boys, and you're not having any."

"It's just ice cream," Tom said at the time.

"Did you fucking hear me?" Frost said.

Frost then grabbed the thirteen-year-old Tom, spun him around, grabbed his arms and twisted one of them right up behind his back, much like a wrestling hammerlock. "He was hurting me," said Tom. "I said, 'Okay, okay!'"

"Not okay," said Frost. "You're a fucking smart aleck and a little fucking prince, aren't you? You need to be taught a couple of lessons. If your parents never taught you any manners, I'm going to teach you."

At that point, and for the first but not last time at Frost's cottage, Tom Jefferson was crying. "Go down to the lake and I don't want to see you in that freezer again," said Frost.

So began a seemingly endless series of hellish days and nights that changed Tom's life forever. What began as a Boy Scout–like

weekend of marshmallow roasts and campfires turned into an introduction to the weird world of David Frost's game playing and mind
control. The torment that began with chastisement over a scoop
of ice cream descended into horrific allegations that sparked an
Ontario Provincial Police investigation. Though charges were never
laid, the police were shocked and disgusted by what they uncovered.
"In thirty-plus years on the job, this was the greatest miscarriage of
justice I had ever been a part of," says an unnamed retired investigating officer. "There was a case to be made against Frost. For
reasons I still to this day don't understand, it never happened."

The OPP viewed the case one way; the Attorney General's
Office viewed it another. The disagreement between police and the
Crown resulted in several heated meetings, at least one of which
had to be interrupted because the two sides of the law threatened
to come to blows with each other. In the end, it was the silence
of Frost's tight group of hockey-playing boys and the unwillingness of the Crown attorneys that prevented any charges from being
laid. The lead investigating officer, Alec Ovenden, fought about
as strenuously as a cop can to have charges laid. But the Crown—
having interviewed the participants at Frost's cottage, all of whom
shared a similar story, one that accused Tom of exaggerating things
and being party to a prank or initiation—determined there was no
reasonable prospect of conviction. A number of different Crown
prosecutors were involved in the determination—they believed
that Tom's testimony, powerful as it might have been, would not
have held up to cross-examination. And prosecutors believed the
array of witnesses would dispute his claims. There was also a fear
that Frost would be defended by the impressive Ottawa defence
attorney Michael Edelson, who had an intimidating reputation
in legal circles. Tensions between the police and prosecutors grew

to near fist fights in meetings in Toronto because of the Crown's unwillingness to proceed with the case.

"It was my word against theirs," said Tom. "And they weren't supporting my word."

After the incident with the ice cream, the abuse escalated sharply, according to Tom. One night, the group was sitting around and watching television: Frost, Mike Jefferson, Sheldon Keefe, Larry Barron, some girlfriends, and others. "Somehow, we got into a conversation about my parents," said Tom. "Looking back, you can see this is what he did. How he divided people. He wanted to hear from me—my side of it."

Frost said, "Your dad is always fucking drunk. Your mom is always drinking. And they're always beating up on you, eh?"

"I said, no, honestly. My dad likes to drink and my mom likes to have a drink sometimes, but that's all, that's it."

That wasn't enough for Frost. "He said [my] dad's a fucking drunk and a fucking this and a fucking that," said Tom. "And he was going on and on. He was trying to make me feel like my parents were fuck-ups. I kind of disagreed with him. And when I did, he kind of exploded."

"What did I tell you about talking back to me? Your mom and dad are fucking losers, fucking assholes."

"He was always negative, putting them down," said Tom. "And I'd look over at my brother, trying to get him to help me out, but I'd get nothing. Frost would say something and he'd say that's how it is. I just wanted the conversation to end so after a while, I started giving in and agreed with the group, whatever they said."

The way Tom sees things, that's how Frost tried to get to him.

Frost's boys were trying to make him one of them, most of them estranged from their families, most of them hockey players of some promise, and all of them seemingly together in attitude and thought. "They told me, 'You'd better get out of there while you can,'" said Tom. "'You can't live [at home] any more. You can come with us now.'"

What emerges from Tom's account is a psychological process not unlike joining a cult, or going through army boot camp, where initiates are broken down and humiliated, then put back together in the image of the others in the group. You give up your identity; you are forced to forswear all you hold dear—that's the cost of acceptance from the new group. That's how every member of the group ends up seeing things the same way.

"They called me a little brat and a little shit disturber. And here's the hard part to explain: I didn't want any part of them, but I wanted to fit in."

Every time Tom found himself cornered, he would turn to his brother looking for some kind of support. But every time, when Tom met his brother's gaze, the expression he saw on Mike's face was blank. The eyes of the brother he idolized were vacant now. Mike had played years of elite hockey and was in many ways a man in Tom's eyes, but his brother's gaze showed that something was missing. The brother Tom yearned for, and still yearns for, was gone, even if he didn't completely see it then.

"Even at the cottage, I'd say to him, 'Why don't you want to talk to me or Mom or Dad? We love you, what the hell? What's going on?' He answered once. He said, 'It's too late.' Then he almost corrected himself. He said, 'They're no good. They're no good for you. You've got to get out of there.'

"I would say, 'Why aren't they good for me?' I'd ask that

question. But he wouldn't answer. I never got his outlook on that. It never made sense to me. It still doesn't."

But as Tom tried to draw his brother back into their family, the peer group at the cottage continued to corrode that bond. He sees that now from the perspective of the confused and angry twenty-three-year-old he has grown into. It hurts now even to look back. To a thirteen-year-old, it can only have been the purest torment.

One morning, according to Tom, he woke up hungry to the enticing smell of French toast emanating from the kitchen. Frost and his wife, Bridget, were cooking and told everyone to come and get it. Everyone didn't necessarily mean everyone.

"When they said that, I ran over there and threw two pieces on my plate," said Tom. "I got the two pieces, came back, and sat down." For some reason, Adam Keefe (Sheldon's younger brother) was laughing. A couple of the other guys were looking at Tom also, their expression saying "you shouldn't have done that."

Then Frost came out of the kitchen and shouted at Tom: "Who the fuck do you think you are? You're the youngest here. You wait till the fucking end."

"I'm sorry," said Tom, and he offered his food back to Frost.

Frost picked up the French toast and spat "this big thick one" right into the middle of it and said, "Now fucking eat it."

"I said, 'No.'"

Frost grabbed Tom's head and slammed his face into the plate. "Fucking eat it!" he screamed.

So Tom Jefferson ate it, or tried to eat it. "I went to the washroom and I was feeling sick. I was disgusted by it, so I didn't finish it."

Frost didn't stop there. "You took all that and you didn't fucking finish it?"

"You spit in it," Tom said.

"I don't need anybody talking back."

"He grabbed me, picked me up, put my arms against my back, and pushed me against the wall. He was really aggressive. I was crying. I called out to Mike. 'Mike, are you going to let him do this to me?!' Mike was just sitting there like it didn't phase him. That made me feel really uncomfortable."

Though Mike may not deserve a great deal of sympathy for his role in his brother's humiliation, his mask of indifference must have hidden at least some remorse, some self-loathing. To escape his own conscience, perhaps his only option was to immerse himself more fully in the tilting, grotesque world of his self-styled mentor. But that kind of repression was of no help to Mike's kid brother. Tom went to his bedroom and Frost told him not to come out "unless I was prepared to get a beating." Tom stayed in his room until he finally drifted off to sleep.

On another day, Tom was down by the lake in the afternoon when Frost offered him $5 on a dare if he would climb up a tree and along a branch that hung over the water. Everyone got involved in the sport, according to Tom. A lot of the other boys started upping the reward if Tom accepted the dare. In another context, at another lake, the goading and chiding of a young teenager would have been no more than some harmless fun. It might have even been the sort of male bonding Tom was there to soak up. But that wasn't what Frost had in store for Tom.

"I'm in the tree and the branch is kind of wobbly and all of a sudden, Dave pulls out a [pellet] rifle and points it at me," said Tom. "The tree is wobbling and I'm getting nervous about it and he tells me to keep climbing across or he's going to shoot me. He took a couple of shots and missed me. He took another shot that hit the branch right in front of my face. So I'm hanging on as best I can and trying to follow along all the way to the end, and he's got this gun pointed at me, and I held on to the branch as long as I could before falling into the shallow water.

"Nobody gave me any money. They all laughed about it. Dave was still pointing the gun at me. I didn't move. Once again, I couldn't believe my brother was standing right there and letting these clowns do this to me, embarrass me, and he didn't do a thing about it."

The days went on and no one seemed to speak up about what was being done to little Tom Jefferson and all that was going on around him—maybe because they had all been through this before in one way or another. Perhaps Frost had faced the same kind of torment when he was younger.

Tom's version of events is the account of a troubled young man haunted by something he couldn't understand. Perhaps the years have honed his story into something more accusatory. Perhaps he's forgotten some of the mitigating moments. But if even half of his story is true, it serves as the clearest, most chilling portrait of how Frost took kids from their homes, entertained them, engaged them, turned them against their families, introduced them to sexual situations, embarrassed them, bullied them. How, in his own words, he "initiated" them; encouraged drinking under age, sexual sharing, and public touching; and participated himself in both verbal and physical abuse.

One night, according to Tom, it was sex talk and inappropriate touching; on another, it was drinking. Before going to Frost's cottage, "I don't believe I'd ever had a drink and certainly I hadn't been drunk," Tom said. His parents had been concerned about Tom being exposed to alcohol at the cottage. Despite the assurances of Larry Barron, the oldest and most mature of the Frost gang, that underage drinking would never happen, it did. "One night, we're playing a drinking game called Kings," said Tom. "And they were forcing me to have beer after beer, one after another. And I kept hearing, 'Get Tommy another beer. Tommy, get us a beer. Tommy, get yourself a beer.' I was getting intoxicated for the first time and eventually I threw up all over myself, in my bed. Dave had the boys come and take me in the shower and shower me. I can't remember if the boys were nude, but I was."

When Tom woke up the next morning, there were drawings on his ankles and he was told that while he was sleeping some of the boys had "stuck Q-tips with Icy Cold up my ass." There were drawings all over Tom's legs and face. "They made a mockery of me while I was sleeping," said Tom. "It was scary. Because I didn't know what else they had done.

"They said they did some things to me but I don't know what really happened. I was thinking the worst, though."

And by then, he had reason to suspect the worst.

To a thirteen-year-old, teasing and bullying is terrifying and cruel. To be tormented by those you look up to is shattering. But even more horrifying is to be thrust into the world of adult sexuality when it is bewilderingly foreign. There is a reason that the cruellest torture always seems to descend into sexual debasement—because the privacy of sexuality is the last vestige of innocence. After all that Tom had been through, there was further humiliation in store for him.

"One night, we're sitting around and Frost is checking everyone's emails on the computer and somehow the topic of 'banging broads' came up. Frost said to me in front of everybody, 'I bet you have a small dick like your brother, eh?'"

Tom was embarrassed and didn't say a thing.

"Go ahead," Frost said. "Show us."

"Before I could do anything he pulled me by my shorts over to him, and reached his hands down my pants and grabbed a hold of my dick and just held on to it. I was thinking, 'Fuck, what is going on here?' Like what are you supposed to think? I looked at my brother again and again I got no reaction. It was like everything was normal. Like this was normal? And then Frost said, 'Well, Sheldon [Keefe] has a pretty big cock. Why don't you pull it out and show Tommy what a real dick looks like.'"

On instruction, according to Tom, Sheldon, today a junior-hockey owner, operator, and coach himself, pulled down his pants and displayed his penis. "And he stood there until Dave told him it was okay to put it back. At this point, he [Dave] was still holding on to mine and I had my hand on his hand, indicating 'Let go,' but he didn't acknowledge it at all. And there were a couple of girls there also, watching. You can't imagine what I was feeling."

At the time, Frost's wife, Bridget, wasn't around. "She knew better than to say anything, anyhow," said Tom. "One time, she said, 'That's enough!' when he was doing something. And he said, 'Why don't you go downstairs and stick your big tit in Ty's mouth again.'"

The bizarre sexuality became more and more of a feature of the group's evenings. Another night at the cottage, sitting around near the pool table, somebody put some music on the CD player. "They [the boys] told me to start dancing," said Tom.

"Frost said, 'Take your clothes off. Get on the pool table, and start dancing.'

"He was giving me orders," said Tom. "The guys were shitting themselves laughing.... And the whole time, he had a rifle on me. He said if I didn't take my clothes off, he would shoot me. And after I took my clothes off, I just stood there—I wasn't dancing. I was just standing there on the pool table looking embarrassed, so after a while, I jumped down."

"You're not fucking done," said Frost. And then Frost ordered Tom to go to his room. "Go back to your fucking room until you learn some manners."

Another night, with the group sitting around, Frost asked Tom directly, "Do you want to have sex?"

He didn't mean with him. He sent Tom to Sheldon Keefe's room. "He's fucking his girlfriend right now," said Frost. "Why don't you step in and finish."

"I went to Sheldon's room. At this point, I wasn't going to question Dave any more. I wasn't going to ask why any more, I was just going to do it. So I went to Sheldon's room and he was fucking his girlfriend. Sheldon got up, came out of the room, and I followed him out."

"What the fuck are you doing?" Frost yelled, when he saw Tom. "Get back in there and finish the job."

"I'm not doing that. That's Sheldon's girlfriend."

At that point, Frost called Tom Jefferson a "fucking pussy."

"Then he told me to go downstairs. 'Go downstairs and help your brother out. He'll need it.' So I go downstairs and my brother had gone out the other door. I walk into the room and the girl says, 'Mike?'"

"Nope."

"Tommy," she shrieked. "What the fuck. Get out of here."

Tom Jefferson went back upstairs only to be called a pussy once again by Frost.

That wasn't the only time Frost attempted to have Jefferson lose his virginity. In another night at the cottage, he told Sheldon's girlfriend to show her naked body to Tom. Bizarrely, she was sitting on a couch wrapped only in a blanket. When she stood up and let the blanket slip, Frost said, "Don't you want that? Go fuck that. You two, go."

Tom admits to being mesmerized by her attractive body.

"I think she would have," said Tom. "She did that kind of thing. I wasn't ready for it. For some reason, I just remember seeing a butterfly tattoo on her upper thigh, near the lower stomach area. I was staring at it, kind of fixated on it. She had a great body. I just said, 'No. I can't.'"

The daily attempts to initiate Tom Jefferson didn't stop, according to Tom. It is impossible to know how much was a concerted effort, and how much was the spontaneous coercive pressure of a large group; how much was pure and deliberate malice, and how much was just the dim-witted cruelty of young men who knew no other way to be together. The most generous interpretation is that this closed circle of guys who had been together for years had become so desensitized to brutality that they were incapable of noticing the effect they were having on the impressionable thirteen-year-old in their midst.

But to make this kind of excuse on their behalf means placing the blame more squarely on Frost. Frost was responsible not only because it was his cottage, but also because he was their mentor. He was perfectly happy to take credit for their successes on and off the ice, so it seems only fair to look to him to see how these young men had become so heedlessly cruel.

Whether the efforts to break Tom were fully deliberate or not, what cannot be doubted is their sickening effectiveness. As scared and humiliated as he was, as weary of betrayal as he had become, he wanted more than ever to fit in. "I hated Dave but I kind of liked him, too. That's the weird part.... For some reason, Dave was nice sometimes and he would talk to you and listen to you, and then he'd be this complete asshole.

"I can see how you can get trapped in all this, but I didn't want to get trapped."

What he didn't know was that he *was* trapped. He just didn't realize it until he tried to break free. He wanted to talk to his parents. He missed them, needed them. He wanted to call home. But, just like the ice cream, the phone was off limits. When he asked to call home, Frost told him to go down to the lake, that they'd call later. So he did—what else could he do? When he came back inside, Frost told him he'd called the Jeffersons. Everything was fine, he said. But his parents would be going away for a while, so Tom would be staying at the cottage for another week.

"My heart just dropped," says Tom. "'Now what?' I thought. I'm thinking, 'Are you serious?' I really wanted to call them." Just when Tom had looked to escape, he learned that he was trapped for another week. He found out later that Frost told his parents Tom was having such a fun time that he didn't have time to call, so Frost was calling on his behalf.

According to Frost, Tom was having the time of his life and it would have been a shame not to have him stay for another week. Just what the Jeffersons were hoping to hear.

That is the heartbreaking irony of the trauma that changed the course of Tom Jefferson's life: his parents, thinking and hoping that they were doing the right thing, thrust their son into the deranged orbit of a man they trusted.

But there would be no such thing as betrayal in the world if there were no such thing as trust.

For the same reason many hockey parents rely on coaches, the Jeffersons relied on Frost. He was a good coach—nobody could dispute that. And he had the results to prove it.

But the Jeffersons trusted him further than his hockey knowledge would warrant. They trusted him with something more cherished than even their dream that Mike would play in the NHL. They trusted him to fix their family.

It was not until years had passed that they would come to realize that it was Frost who had sabotaged it in the first place. But by then, it would be much too late. Too late, Steve Jefferson came to realize that he had trusted the wrong guy, for the wrong reason.

"The second week at the cottage, the problems escalated. You never expect these things to happen to you. You read about it, you hear about it, but you'd never wish this on anybody. Never."

One night, Tom came to think he might earn his brother's respect if he just did what he was told. "That's how misguided you can get in all this," he said. "You don't know what to think. You're trying to make sense of something that doesn't make sense. Everybody was in my bedroom and I'm being taped to the bunk beds with duct tape. And as they're doing this, Frost rips my shorts down again. He starts taping my ass cheeks, one to one side and the other cheek to the other side so that my ass is wide open. They tape my legs to the bunk bed. I'm pulling away and trying to loosen it and Frost is slapping me and telling me not to pull away. They taped me real good so I couldn't get away at first.

"Then Frost grabbed my penis and taped it around and around. Everyone was laughing, taking pictures, and I know that because the pictures were later found [at Sheldon Keefe's parents' house]. They said they were going to leave the room and they turned the lights off. But nobody left the room, I think. They just stayed there and watched in the dark. And eventually I ripped out of the tape. I just remember how uncomfortable and embarrassing all that felt.

"And what pissed me off is that Mike didn't stand up for me once. To this day, when I look back at those two weeks, and do you know how many times I've gone over this in my head, that's why I have trust issues with everybody around me. I tell my friends now I can't trust them. I tell my girlfriend I can't trust her. It's hard to have relationships. I don't trust anybody. I haven't dealt with it. I haven't got this out of my system. It's sexual abuse. I don't know what else to call it. I haven't dealt with it. I can't deal with it."

To this day, Sue Jefferson still agonizes that she agreed to allow Tom to go to Frost's cottage. "I was sick about it the day he left [for the cottage]. I just had a bad feeling about it.

"When Tom came home from the cottage, he had clearly changed. We weren't sure what had gone on. But when he came home, he started taking his meals and eating downstairs, just like Mike had done at one time. Tom didn't want to talk to us, but I wasn't about to make the same mistakes over again. I wasn't about to stand by and let it happen again.

"It took me three days of bugging him, but I had to talk to him. He had to talk to us. I insisted on it. I knew there was something to get out of him. So after three days of constant badgering, he broke down and starting telling me things.

"Once I started hearing them, I was livid. I didn't know what to do. I wanted to call the police. But what proof did we have? You need proof. Word of mouth from a kid isn't going to do anything and we'd learned from dealing with Dave over the years that that wasn't going to work. You need lots of proof to nail these kinds of guys. Tom was willing to talk and wanted Frost to get arrested. He wanted something done. He knew what happened there wasn't right. He was thirteen years old and he had more guts than any of them."

The courage that helped Tom Jefferson get through those two traumatic weeks has seen him through the many fallout difficulties that have come over the years that followed. But no amount of courage could help even a kid like Tom leave that anger and betrayal behind. There are some things even the strongest among us cannot leave behind.

"I'd like to go away and start [my life] all over again. Dave Frost fucked it up for me, for my family, destroyed it beyond fixing. I haven't been able to get over this. It's ruined my life."

5

Mom's Story

Normally, the bond is unbreakable: a mom and her first-born son. A connection for a lifetime.

But for more than a decade now, Sue Jefferson has not spoken to her oldest son. She hasn't touched him, hasn't hugged him, hasn't had any meaningful contact with him. She can do no more than stand by and watch her son's life unfold. But standing on the sidelines does not mean that Sue Jefferson doesn't care. Ask any NHL hockey player and he will tell you that it's harder to watch his teammates play than it is to be in the game himself. He'll tell you that watching powerlessly as the fate of the people he cares about is played out before his eyes is a special kind of torment. How much harder must it be for a mother to watch not just a hockey game, but whole years come and go?

Sue Jefferson knows the right words, but doesn't know how to put them to the right use. Even a mother, often the linchpin of a household, can be reduced to a powerless witness to her own family's separation and suffering. And in the case of the Jeffersons, what has been left behind? An estranged boy who went to prison.

A depressed mom who lost her sense of herself. A father who drank too much. A youngest son damaged by all he was exposed to. What could Sue Jefferson do once so much that she cherished was taken from her?

She could do nothing.

It would all sound clichéd, sadly scripted for soap opera, if it weren't so inescapably real.

There are no family photographs on the walls of the Jeffersons' modest home in rural Erin, Ontario. They have all been taken down. The scrapbooks have been put away, packed in boxes. Photos have been filed away in envelopes, tucked away in cupboards and rarely opened. This is a house decorated by a family wrenched from its own past, scarcely more personal than a hotel room.

"I can't put them [the photos] up," said Sue. "I just can't. I have to keep the pictures of Mike in a closet in the bedroom. I don't look at them. It hurts too much. The only pictures I ever look at are when he's little. That's the hardest part to remember. He's grown up. He's a man now. And I remember him as this little innocent thing, hunting for Easter eggs. He was so full of energy. He'd climb the walls and he was non-stop.

"And he seemed to take particular pleasure in driving Mommy nuts."

There is barely Christmas any more in the Jefferson home. It's been more than a decade since the four Jeffersons could gather around the tree. Now there are only three of them, and Christmas morning is a reminder that someone the family holds dear is somewhere else, a place they can't even guess. The last time Sue spoke to her son Mike, in early 2000, he was walking out the door with his Christmas gift in his hands. It had taken him three months to come by to pick it up. He claimed his present, a glass chess set, said thank you, stayed a few awkward minutes, and then left. He was on his way to be with David Frost. That was the last "Christmas cheer" the four Jeffersons shared.

Mike Jefferson had yet to change his last name to Danton, but it was clear by that period of Christmas 1999 and the months afterwards that he had already divorced himself from the family. He was nineteen years old. If he can be said to have had a permanent home, it was Frost's, not the Jeffersons'. Of all the shocking things that have come to light in Mike Danton's story, even amid the sordid tales of sex and violence and a murder plot, what is perhaps the most troubling is a young man's willingness to turn his back on the people who love him.

Mike Danton has many admirable qualities. He is hard-working and bright. He has shown himself to be a good student. When he has asked for sympathy, it is sometimes possible to see him as a victim. But it is difficult to extend full sympathy to someone willing to spurn his own mother.

"How do you walk away from your parents, walk away from your mom?" asked Joel Quenneville, who coached Danton in St. Louis and later went on to lead the Chicago Blackhawks to a Stanley Cup.

"How do you do that? As a parent, that has to just eat you away. I don't know if you can ever get over that. I don't know if I would. That has to be the worst thing to ever happen to a parent. How do you live with that? That's just one of the parts of all this I may never understand."

if there is such a thing as a typical hockey mom, Sue Jefferson was not it. She didn't live for her son's next goal, next game, next victory.

She wasn't caught up in what team he played for or how much ice time he received or many of the things that often consumed her husband and her household. At times, with hockey the centre of so much of their lives, she felt like an outsider in her own home, in a family so focused on Mike's burgeoning career. Steve and Mike would go off to the minor-hockey games or practices together; at home, it would be hockey on television, hockey on video-game screens, hockey on the backyard rink—Dad and Mike, with Mom somehow on the outside looking in. She didn't necessarily see that when it was happening, but she sees it now through clearer eyes and the perspective of time.

Sue Jefferson believes she began to lose her son ever so slightly just after Tom was born on March 17, 1987—before there was any association with Frost. She may, in fact, be exaggerating that separation. But when you haven't seen your son in a decade, you examine all the possibilities; you ruminate too often about what went wrong. Mike had not reached his seventh birthday by the time of Tom's birth. "Like a lot of first-borns, Mike starting acting jealous when Tom was born," said Sue. "I noticed a change in him right away but you don't really think of it as anything at the time. You don't think it will last. It happens with a lot of kids when a younger sibling is born. It's like a territorial reaction. You figure it will be there for a little while and then it will disappear. That's what first-borns do.

"I would be breastfeeding and I was the shy type—I wouldn't do it in front of everybody the way some moms will. So I would go up to the bedroom and breastfeed Tom, and Mike would be yelling, 'Mom, Mom!' from downstairs and I wouldn't answer him.

"During nursing, I was separated a lot from Mike. I probably should have been more open. I should have done it right in front of him. I should have involved him somehow. But from then, way back then, I started to see that he was pulling away from me, that he was jealous of Tom, that I was always with the baby. The trust wasn't the same. And by that time he was playing hockey, so there was a natural separation of sorts. Dad and Mike would go off to the game. Mom and Tom would stay home. I didn't see any of this back then. I really didn't think it was important. I just found it easier for me to be home than out at some cold rink with a baby."

Minor hockey at the highest level is a five-times-a-week commitment, so Sue was at home alone with Tom quite often. And when Tom was old enough and interested enough in the game, he would go along with his dad. Soon, it was just Sue at home. She hated the drives to and from the rink, from Brampton into Toronto, with the entire topic of conversation being that night's game.

She didn't, she says now, understand boys or care that much for hockey. The hockey obsession she was surrounded by was completely foreign to her. She had grown up in a strict Eastern European expat culture, the daughter of Charlie and Luba Gebe, part Hungarian, part Ukrainian, in a house full of girls. What did she know of boys' testosterone-fuelled dreams? She cared for family. She was resolute about that. Family was everything to her.

"I grew up with sisters," said Sue. "The guys' world was always different for me. Steve would always say to leave it alone, let Mike be, this is how guys do things. This is male bonding."

But when the male bonding started to include David Frost, Sue began to feel even more left out. She saw her family reconfiguring, and she didn't like the shape it was taking. Long before there were any outward signs of trouble, Sue Jefferson had an instinct, maybe a mother's instinct, that no one else in the family shared. She seemed to know and understand the problems in her life before anyone else saw them coming. But too often, she didn't know how to act on them or what to do about them. And even when she did, she had no family support for her thoughts.

She strongly disliked David Frost almost from the moment she first met him. She didn't care for what she called his rude behaviour and arrogance. She found him impossible to trust. And that lack of trust ultimately damaged the bond between mother and child and injured the relationship between wife and husband. Because she didn't fall under the spell that allowed Frost to manipulate both Steve and Mike, Sue became an outsider, her warnings increasingly unwelcome and unheeded.

Very suddenly, Sue had lost control of the thing she cared about most: her family. If she tried to steer Steve away from this new coach, he would dismiss her on the grounds that she knew nothing about hockey. The result was corrosive. The more Sue stood up for her family, the more the Jeffersons fought.

"Dave was right about one thing," said Sue. "There was always arguing, fighting going on in our house. A lot of fighting, a lot of hollering, a lot of tension.

"What he doesn't say? The arguments were all about him."

But if Frost made Sue and Steve's marriage difficult, he made her relationship with her son all but impossible. While Mike may tell stories about the abuse he suffered from his father, what he has never mentioned to anyone is the verbal abuse he heaped upon his mother. It got to a point, in Mike's teenage years, where he was always cold, nasty, withdrawn, and abusive to his mother. This wasn't anything like the usual set-tos that occur between hormonal teens and their parents. That is expected in most homes. Kids assert themselves. But Mike Jefferson went far, far beyond that. He would call her all kinds of names. Lesbian. Bitch. If a word could hurt, he would use it. The fights were a constant, and discipline was impossible. When words couldn't cow her, Mike would intimidate her physically, pushing back his shoulders and flexing his chest.

"It got to the point where I couldn't touch him any more," said Sue. "He wouldn't let me. He was maybe fourteen, fifteen years old. I would touch him on the shoulder and he would completely lose it. Imagine that feeling for a mother. You have no idea what that feels like. Imagine trying to get a hug and having your own child turn away. Imagine touching your son and having him act like he's offended by you.

"I would say something to Michael and he would say, 'Shut up. Mind your own business.' Or he'd say, 'Go to your room, you lesbian.'" And if the argument got too heated, no matter what it was about, he would threaten, "I'll never fucking see you again."

And that was the signal, in Sue's mind, to back away. Arguing, Sue thought, was better than losing him altogether.

That was Mike's trump card. If all else failed, he could use his mother's love against her. He could threaten to leave. Sue Jefferson could live with the fights inside her house, with the tumult outside her house, so long as her family, or what was left of it, was together. But what she had trouble with—what they all had trouble with— were the constant threats. Mike Jefferson was forever telling them that David Frost did all the things for him that they never did; that he gave more of himself than they ever did; that if they didn't like the way he was, he'd leave. You don't know what you're doing, Mike would say, Dave knows. He can get me there. You can't.

"Mike was almost sixteen at the time," said Sue. "Legally, he could leave at almost any time. We knew that." Emotionally, he was already gone from the family.

"Mom would just break down and cry," said Tom Jefferson of the arguments. "It was horrible."

That was Mike Jefferson at his worst. And while his behaviour in his teenage years may have been exemplary for his coaches and teachers—for any authority figures outside the home—it was not that way around his family.

All Sue Jefferson could hold on to was a mother's desperate hope. Whatever had turned him against his family, he'd grow out of it. Steve believed that to be true. He counted on it, and he convinced the family it would heal. Sue wasn't so certain. But she clung to Steve's optimism. Really, what choice did she have? When he said, "I'll never fucking see you again," the worry was that when he turned sixteen, he would leave. So without a solution, and with Steve backing Frost as Mike's hockey mentor, the two would argue. The house had turned into something of a verbal war zone.

"We would argue," Sue said. "Steve would defend Frost and I would be upset. But I was losing Michael. I knew that. A mother sees that. A mother feels that.

"We would fight over almost everything and it was constant. I'd ask [Mike] what's wrong and he'd say nothing. He was silent a lot, and if he wasn't silent, there would be these outbursts. There was almost nothing in between. He'd say something like, 'You don't know what you're talking about. [Frost's] done more for me than you guys ever have or ever will. You don't know anything.' And I'd be thinking, 'I'm just a woman. Stupid. I'm just stupid.' He'd call me a lesbian. He'd call me this or that. Anything derogatory. I'd cry sometimes, and sometimes I'd get right in his face. I tried different ways of dealing with him. And he'd be looking down at me with all that muscle, and there wasn't much I could do. The emotion of going through this with your son is devastating. But I never wanted to let it sit. I always needed a solution.

"Before he went to bed, I'd grab a bar of soap sometimes and I'd write something on the mirror in his bathroom. A message to him. Something. Just so when he woke up in the morning, the first thing he'd see was my words. I was forever leaving him a note of some kind. I found that easier than talking to him. I wanted him to know … your mother loves you.

"By the time he got to Quinte, I couldn't give him hugs any more. I knew that. One day, I said jokingly to him, 'Can we at least shake hands?' He wouldn't shake my hand. You have no idea what that felt like. I can't even explain it. His grandparents would go to games, his cousins, and he wouldn't take the time to acknowledge them. It was like he wasn't human any more. He was completely distant. Imagine, you see your son, but it's not really him."

How much of this tension was normal teenage angst and how much was the influence of Frost is impossible to determine. But while no one save for Frost knows his motives, what emerges is a pattern in which time and again, Frost came between his young player and the player's parents. One time, Mike's paternal grandfather attended one of his junior games, and he introduced himself to Frost. "I don't give a fuck who you are," said Frost. "You're not seeing him."

When Jefferson family members died, Mike would be conspicuously absent from the funerals. Frost wouldn't allow him to go. "That was sick to me," said Sue. "He used to love his family. He loved when the whole family was around. And then this."

What seemed strange in a household where strange was the norm, was how much time Frost spent with Jefferson, even if he happened to be fourteen years older than Mike.

"Dave would come by and take [Mike and] the boys to the movies a lot," says Tom Jefferson. "I didn't think of it at the time, really, but when you think of it now, what fourteen-year-old do you know who would want to go the movies with their twenty-eight-year-old hockey coach? Isn't that a little off? And what twenty-eight-year-old coach hangs around with a bunch of fourteen-year-olds?"

It was particularly weird to Sue Jefferson, but as the years passed, her self-esteem chipped away, and her self-confidence ebbed to the point that she realized she had completely lost control not only of her family, but also of her house.

"One time, Dave and the boys came over at about two in the morning and I would always defend Dave," Steve Jefferson said. "They brought this girl with them and she couldn't have been any older than fourteen, I think. And from my understanding, some of the boys were downstairs having their way with her. And Sue says to me, 'Get down there and put a stop to this.'

"I said, 'Leave it alone.' And, foolishly, I just let it be. This was kid stuff, I thought. I just wiped my mind blank of the whole thing. I would defend Dave. But honestly, what was an adult doing in a basement with teenaged boys and girls having sex? How did I let this happen in my own house? I can't believe I was party to this."

Sue Jefferson wasn't so calm about what was going on in her basement. "I made noise, lots of noise. I hollered and screamed. I was at the top of the stairs making comments and Michael would come up partway and say, 'Shut up' or 'Mind your own business' or 'Go to your room, you lesbian.' And when I was still yelling, he'd threaten, 'I'll never fucking see you again.'"

Years later, after Mike had left home and wrenched himself from his family, a call came in on the Jeffersons' answering machine. Sue wouldn't or couldn't erase it for the longest time. She would play it back and listen and play it for others and discuss. The message was cryptic, a child's words in a man's voice. The voice on the phone, a voice she believed to be her son Mike's, begged, "Help us." Two words on an answering machine. Then a hang-up.

He never called again.

She never verified that the voice belonged to Mike, but she is certain to this day that it was him. She is certain it was a rare cry for help.

But not long after the call, Dave Frost called the Jefferson home. That's the way it was with Frost. "It was obvious to me, Mike was reaching out to us, for whatever reason," said Sue. "He was trying to reach out and Dave cut him off. I think every once in a while, he would come to his senses and want to come home. I believe that to be true; I have to believe that. But he didn't know how to do it.

"After getting that 'Help us' call, Dave called completely out of the blue and he said, 'I just wanted to talk to Steve' and stuff like that. And they'd have a conversation, like nothing wrong was going on.

"That message still haunts me today. I'm sorry I ever erased it. That was a message I wanted to play for the police, but what was I going to tell them? They wouldn't be able to identify who it was. There was no crime committed. What could I tell them? What could I do?"

Instead, she listened to the message over and over. "It was talking to me. I believe that. I knew what it was saying. I wish I could have done something about it. Mike hasn't reached out very often in his life, but when he has, he's usually [been] cut off. I'd like to think he was trying to send us some kind of message. Later, he did the same thing in St. Louis. He was trying to separate himself from Dave Frost. And look what happened to him. He ended up going to jail."

The day that Susan Gebe decided that Steve Jefferson was the man for her happened to be one of the most frightening days in Canadian high-school history. Before there was Columbine in Colorado, there was Brampton Centennial just outside Toronto. And on May 28, 1975, Michael Slobodian, a student whom Susan and Steve both knew, pulled out two rifles, killed a teacher and a fellow student, and wounded thirteen other students, before ending his shooting spree by taking his own life with his gun.

"We were close enough to it that we had speckles of blood on the back of our clothes," said Sue. "There were bullets flying off the walls and chunks of mortar all over and people were screaming. I still remember looking down and there was a teacher lying on the ground beside my locker. It was terrible.

"Everybody's running and panicking and crying and I feel this arm on me. Steve pulled me out of the school, almost dragging me as I'm wearing these great big platform shoes. And as I get out of the school, I'm thinking, 'Oh wow, he saved my life. He put my life ahead of his own.' It was kind of heroic.

"Steve took me outside the school, then he went back in, looking for his sister. He was like the only guy taking charge. When he got back in the hall, they halted him. At first, they [police] thought he might have been involved. But after a second or so, they had him working with them; they had him get down and hold a sheet of plastic over the abdomen of this teacher— there was a big hole in his stomach. Steve was trying to save the teacher's life."

Steve Jefferson never went back to school after that day. For whatever reason, he couldn't or wouldn't. But under the most frightening of circumstances, with lives lost, lives on the line, and foreshadowing a life of controversy and difficulty that would follow them, Sue Jefferson had fallen in love with this man who had put her life before his own. They became close at the crime scene, if they weren't already. First, they trusted each other, then loved each other. Two years later, they would be married. Thirty-four years later, after all they have been through, in a world where half the marriages don't make it, and their family life has been somewhat destroyed, they are miraculously and incredibly still together. Sue believes in family. It may be her strongest belief. While they are opposites in every conceivable way, they have stayed together through the worst periods of their life, through losing their son; watching him go to prison; through Steve's drinking and occasional bouts with the law; at times losing themselves; dealing with the tumult of Tom; a mom's depression; financial difficulty; and the regular rigours that marriage can bring. Most marriages could not have survived all of that. Many wouldn't weather even a small part of that hardship. Somehow, the Jeffersons have made it.

"I didn't think we would last, because that [Frost] was all we fought about and because you start laying guilt on each other. And it's all we talked about. I mean *all* we talked about. It was consuming our lives. And all I ever said was, 'You should have listened to me. You should have trusted me.'

"At times, our family was all together, the three of us, but we had to go our separate ways just to get away from it all. Sometimes, it hasn't been easy. It's changed us; it's changed us all. I used to be a happy person, full of life, full of fun. I'm not that happy person I used to be. I've been depressed on and off. I've had trouble getting out of bed some days. I don't trust people the way I used to. I have mood swings. Tom doesn't trust people. He has anger issues.

"For a long time, I couldn't get out of bed. I couldn't go to work. And when I went to work, I wasn't me. I was being rude to customers. If you're driving a coffee truck and a customer would say, 'You've got no fruit cup today,' I would just lash out at him and say, 'Fruit cup? I've got bigger problems than a fruit cup. You're worried about a fucking fruit cup?'

"I'm on the job and I realize I was starting to lose a sense of myself, who I was. I was blowing up at people. That wasn't me. I had to stop working because it wasn't good for me. Work wasn't good, but being at home, that wasn't good either.

"I slept and slept and slept. I went on antidepressants, went off them. I thought, 'I don't want pills. I want somebody to talk to.'" But even trying to find the right person proved to be frustrating. Sue would wait too long for appointments, too long between appointments. It wasn't working. She had little patience. Like a lot of people, she needed an instant solution. "When it's your life that's falling apart, it's difficult to be patient."

She went to one doctor who told her that his father had lived through the Holocaust and had seen terrible things in his life. He got over it, the doctor told her, so she could, too. "That's what he said to me. His view was, *Get over it*. That was it. Just get over it."

But there is really no way to get over something that is never over. It is healthy to grieve and then come to peace with the absence of a loved one who is truly gone. That is all anyone can hope for in the wake of a terrible loss. But it is all but impossible to find that peace when the departure of the loved one seems calculated to wound you.

"When we'd go to Quinte to watch him play junior hockey, there would be almost no contact between us and him," says Sue.

"But if Bridget [Frost] was around with her baby, he'd be carrying it around, with a big smile on his face. It was almost like he would carry the baby and parade around with him, to hurt Tom and me." It was as though Mike was creating a parody of a family to taunt his parents and make clear how totally Frost had replaced them in his life.

Or maybe there was another reason.

There are people in the National Hockey League familiar with Mike, as well as police officers in Ontario and both Steve and Sue, who believe Mike may be the biological father of one of David Frost's children. The story has been around for some time. That startling connection may help to resolve some of the unanswered questions about the relationship between Frost and the young man who would become infamous under the name Mike Danton—and how they cannot separate, even after Danton tried to have Frost murdered.

"I was told that Mike is the dad by the police and I've been told that by other people, too," the emotional mother says, trying to compose herself. But the first time she heard the shocking news, whether it's true or not, came when she was out on business. "I was driving the coffee truck and I bumped into a construction worker who is the best friend of Bridget's brother. The guy said to me, 'You're Sue Jefferson. Michael's your son, right? I'm Bridget's brother's best friend and we're really sorry to hear about this and the whole family is upset and devastated by this, but are you aware that Michael is the father of that baby?'"

Sue said she just froze momentarily and even as she retells the story she remains almost frozen in shock. "Can you imagine hearing that when you're on a job site? Can you imagine hearing something like that at all, and from a stranger? I'm thinking, 'My

God. That's my son. I'm a grandmother and I don't even know it.'
And all these thoughts are racing through your head. Is this true?
You don't know what to think. And why would anyone be telling
me this if it wasn't true?

"Is it true? I don't know. But I believe it to be true. The baby
looked just like Mike. And I've heard it from enough different
people now, enough people to believe it to be true. I know there
are a lot of things we're not sure about. But I do know that Dave
likes to have everybody in bed with everybody. That's what he does,
so you know maybe this is possible." (Asked for the purposes of
this book whether there is truth to these rumours, Mike Danton
refused to respond.)

Absorbing crazy revelations from strangers while at at work;
seeing her son's notorious name in the headlines; arguing at the
kitchen table over what went so wrong and when; supporting her
youngest son when he stumbles; addressing her own depression—
Sue Jefferson is in no position to "get over" anything. With eyes a
soggy red from years of crying, she lives every day with the fallout of
a seemingly inconsequential minor-hockey decision made years ago.

The side effects of Sue's depression have been many, not the least
of which is her inability and unwillingness to make love any more.
She just can't find her way to enjoy one of the pleasures of life. After
hearing all the Frost stories over the years; listening to rumours
and courtroom testimony; being exposed to too much over too
many years; seeing too much; hearing too much, the thought of
the intimacy of physical love has been tarnished for Sue. She can
love but not make love. She can be warm but doesn't necessarily
require any embrace. Every aspect of her life has been invaded by
the circumstances surrounding the estrangement of Mike from the
family and the sordid, murky manipulations of David Frost.

"Dave's ruined that for me," said Sue. "I think of sex as something dirty now. I can't think of it any other way. I'm sorry … sorry that happened."

Having been let down by the courts, by the hockey establishment, by their best friends, by almost everyone they trusted or turned to for help, Sue has thought about what she could do, what else she could have done. She has no real answers. But sometimes she, like the rest of her family, thinks of killing Frost. His death, she believes, would bring some kind of peace to the Jefferson family.

"The justice system should have taken care of all this," said Sue. "Instead, you have good people thinking of committing murder. Really, that's what it has come to in our lives.

"We all felt like we wanted to do it at one point. I think each of us—me, Steve, Tom—has thought about it. I want to kill Dave, but will I do it? No. I don't want to go to jail. Unfortunately, that runs in our family. We want to kill this man. We want him dead for what he's done to us."

And after everything that's gone on, she still wants her oldest son back. She isn't sure it will ever happen. But she can't stop believing that one day they will be reunited. And what then?

"My stomach would be doing knots, butterflies," said Sue. "If I ever got the chance to see Mike again—starting fresh. I still think about trying to write him a letter but it hurts because I know he's going to push me away. And how many times can you have your heart broken? My heart has been broken to pieces already. Sometimes I feel like those letters that got returned from prison, all torn into little pieces. I'm trying to move on. I have to forget. I still cry every day. Mike's on my mind every day. I still think he's connected to me. I have to think that. I'm his mom."

6

Dad's Story

It is not so much a fantasy but a daily part of Steve Jefferson's reality: He would like to kill David Frost. He would like to see him dead.

That isn't a joke. That isn't idle chatter. This is what he feels inside. The anger is very real. The family he envisioned is in ruins. And it seems apples don't fall very far from trees. At some point in time, his estranged son, Mike Danton, made a similar determination and wound up behind bars for his clumsy attempt to remove David Frost from his life in St. Louis. Steve Jefferson knows there is at least one difference between him and his son: if he had set out to kill Frost, the job would have been completed.

"I think if a doctor told Steve he had two weeks to live, and he got to do whatever he wanted to do with the rest of his life, the first thing on his list would be to kill Frost," says Sue Jefferson. "I know I've thought about it myself. I know Tom's thought about it. We've talked about it. Imagine that, a family sitting around talking about something like this. And just because you think about it and talk about it doesn't mean you're going to do it.

"But with Steve, it's there a lot of the time. It eats away at him. I think I've talked him out of doing something a few times—maybe not killing him, but doing something. I think others have, too. A few times, I wasn't so sure. Many times, I thought he was going to do something crazy. And I'd say him to him, 'Please don't do that. Please don't ruin our lives.'"

Their lives were absolutely entangled yet connected by their hatred of Frost, each family member in their own way considering his demise. Each one of them worried that one of the others would act out of turn.

"And then you take a step back and you think, 'Look what's happened to me.'" said Sue. "Look what's happened to our family? Look what he's done to us, what this has done to all of us. I'm a law-abiding person. Yeah, we've had some problems. Everybody has problems, but mostly we're good people. We've been let down so much by everyone—the courts, the criminal justice system, hockey, the NHL Players' Association, Bob Goodenow, everybody—that this is what you're left with.

"You get good, law-abiding people thinking about murder."

"I think about it," Steve Jefferson said almost matter-of-factly. He was the one who introduced Frost into their lives. That guilt is there. That guilt may never leave him. He not only introduced him, but he was also Frost's leading advocate in his home. Steve supported Frost's abusive coaching because he was witness to how Mike was developing as a hockey player. He blindly supported the close relationship Frost had with Mike. He thought there was a purpose to it all that would come out in the end. He once said in a 1999 interview with the *Toronto Sun*, "Dave Frost is the best thing to ever happen to my kid." He believed it when he said it. He can't believe now what a fool he's been.

That's part of what makes him so bloody angry.

"I think about it a lot [killing him]. Sometimes, I just think of driving to Georgetown [the small Ontario town where Frost sometimes lives] and going to No Frills and waiting for him. I think, 'I'm going to pick up a can of something in one of the aisles, come from behind him, and smash it over his head.' You don't know how many times I've thought of that. At one time, going back, I just wanted him arrested. That was all. And that's all I thought about and I was kind of consumed by it. I wanted what was coming to him. I wanted him to pay for what he'd done to so many people. And if I see him, I'm going to drive [the can] right at him. First time I see him, I'm going to get arrested. I know that. I have no problems going to jail for beating up Dave Frost. Every time I see him, like when he was in court in Napanee, I want to beat him up.

"Look at the families ruined, the relationships ruined. I truly believed in the right way, that he should be taken care of by the legal system. That he would go to jail. That should have happened. I don't believe in the justice system any more. I don't trust it. How could I?

"I don't believe in the police to get anything done. I trusted people. I trusted the police. I trusted the system. I listened to everyone. They told me to let them do their jobs and everything would work out in the end. I believed them all. Where did it get us?

"I still work fifteen hours a day to keep my mind off Dave Frost. People say, 'Why don't you retire?' I can't. I can't sit around and think about this. I can't sit around and think about what's happened to my family. I want to put a bullet through Dave Frost's head. That's the truth. I hate him. I hate the man. Something has to happen to him. One day, if someone comes up to me and tells me that Dave Frost has been murdered, I would celebrate. Believe me, I won't shed any tears for that bastard."

This is an emotional and distraught parent talking. But Steve Jefferson will be the first to tell you that he is no angel. He won't ever be nominated for any father of the year awards. Ward Cleaver he is not. He has warts—all kinds of them. And he has a past. Sue Jefferson may describe herself as law abiding, but it's not an accurate way to portray her husband. Steve has a criminal record and has done time in prison. As much as he wanted to be, he found it difficult to be the ideal dad or husband. He drank—and admittedly still drinks— more than he should. He often would make a spectacle of himself, especially at arenas, although he doesn't necessarily see it that way. He can be verbally abusive and sometimes violent when drinking. And more than anyone else, he will admit a certain responsibility for the fractured home in which he has lived, for providing David Frost with the clear and often unquestioned access as coach and hockey mentor that enabled him to all but kidnap Mike and turn him against his family.

When Mike Jefferson was born in 1980, Steve had already been in and out of trouble. He spent six weeks behind bars for his role in an unsophisticated drug-trafficking scheme. He spent his twenty-fourth birthday locked up. The docket against him includes charges for drunk driving, drug trafficking, assault, and possession of narcotics. In his thirties, he was more than just a triple threat. In all, there are eleven different criminal convictions on his record. "I had to get my act together. It was who I was. My old man drank a lot," said Steve. "I drink. I drink too much. To this day, I still smoke weed. I've done some stupid things. But I don't think any of that makes me a bad person."

On one occasion, after losing weight in prison, he came home to see his family and a very young Mike didn't recognize him. "That can't be my daddy," Mike said at the time. "My daddy's fat."

But for all that was flawed with Steve Jefferson, when it came to his family, there was nothing he wouldn't do for them.

What tears up Steve to this day is how he himself lost his way; how he was a Frost booster; how he was so hard on his son Mike; how he misread so many clues; how his vision was blurred by his chase of the dream; how he refused to listen to his wife's concerns or respect her views; how his focus on Mike's emerging hockey career meant everything to him. He is not the first parent who lost his way, but few have ever lived a life like Steve Jefferson's, with all the sadness and crazy twists and turns.

So much of it started with hockey. The sport meant everything to Steve. He played, coached, analyzed, and even made an outdoor rink in the backyard. He also watched hockey religiously on television; played video games of hockey; and watched hockey films, game films—anything that was hockey. He lived the dream vicariously through both Mike's terrific and emerging talent as well as his own undying commitment to being a hockey dad. Even now, years after losing his son, after Mike has done serious time in prison, after his family has endured so much, he can recall the circumstances and moments from teams and games and youth tournaments of years gone by as if they had happened yesterday. And his face lights up as he tells the stories with relish and rich detail. He can name the rink, the town, the team, the time, the score, even what was going on. It is like time has stopped for Steve Jefferson. Two decades ago, he lost his son, just not his memories,

not what attached them as father and son. He didn't lose the experience of minor hockey, summer tournaments, winter tournaments,
provincial playdowns. The game within the game. Those were his
happiest times.

It was Mike, the budding young hockey star, and Steve, the
barrel-chested dad, proud and perhaps sometimes a bit too loud.
The hockey dad who never missed a game, a meeting, a practice.
Anything. Forever together, he thought. Isn't that what the minor-
hockey experience is supposed to be all about?

If it was hockey, it didn't matter the time, the place, or the cost.
He was there. He was a fixture as a parent on every team Mike
Jefferson played on as a kid.

The coffee truck made him a celebrity dad. There were snacks
for everyone when the kids won. Steve took a certain pride in
being more than just the average team parent who blended into the
background. "Everybody knew me," said Steve. "I was like the lead
dad on almost every team."

In many ways, that was all he ever wanted, all he cared about,
all he talked about: to be the dad of a son going places in hockey.

By the time Mike was thirteen years old, less than three years
after meeting David Frost for the first time, Steve had that unmistak-
able feeling: "Mike was going to play in the NHL. I truly believed
that. You could see he had something the other kids didn't have.
Something inside of him." It may have been his son's game, but this
was clearly a shared dream. Mike said it at the age of six. His father
saw there was more to the young boy's words by the time Mike
was thirteen. "At first, I thought I wanted it more than Mike," said
Steve. "Then it became obvious. Mike wanted it more than me.
When it reached that point, I knew he had what it takes. He would
do anything for hockey. We would do anything for hockey."

"I was what you'd call hockey broke, but I didn't care," said Steve. "We were playing twelve or thirteen tournaments a year, summer and winter. That was easy a grand a weekend. We couldn't afford it but we weren't going to deny him anything. We weren't going to stand in the way of his development. We went into all kinds of debt to make sure he had everything and believe me there were some financial pressures."

So much of Steve Jefferson's adult life has been defined by hockey. When Mike was seven years old, playing for the Chinguacousy Blues, family time never seemed better. Mike was best friends with Sheldon Keefe, his teammate and the best player on the Blues. Brian Keefe and Steve were seemingly inseparable. The senior Keefe was from Prince Edward Island and had many of the down-home qualities Jefferson, who is part Maritimer, admired. And neither of them ever met a hockey game, an arena bar, or a late night they didn't like.

The two men lived within walking distance of each other, and would gather nightly at Jefferson's Brampton home. They would go through a case of beer; watch whatever NHL games were on TV that night; and talk about their families, kids, and the growing hockey careers of their youngsters. They were all going places, they thought. Hockey families on the rise. Sheldon Keefe was the most skilled hockey player on almost every team he played on. He was the kid everybody talked about. Mike Jefferson was the hardest-working kid—the kid who made things happen. They were all close friends. The families vacationed together. The situation couldn't have been better.

"I didn't have to look for Brian. I always knew where he was," said Steve. "He was at my house, drinking beer and watching hockey. That's what we did. We became best friends. The boys became best friends. The four of us would do everything together. And later on, with his son Adam, and my son Tom, the four of us went to Florida together. It was that tight a relationship. I thought everything was going great in our lives."

The skills of Sheldon Keefe and to a lesser extent Mike Jefferson attracted minor-hockey coaches looking to make their teams better. One of the coaches they attracted was a well-known operator of a Brampton hockey school named David Frost.

"The first time I really met Frost, he was recruiting for a Young Nats team he was going to coach. I kind of knew who he was by reputation. He ran a hockey school not far from us and was known for really pushing players. I kind of liked that. I thought Mike needed that.

"Frost came up to me and said, 'If you get Mike to play for me, I'll make him captain of the team.' For a hockey dad, that was quite an introduction and an enticement. It's not unusual for minor-hockey coaches to use recruiting tactics, such as promising heavy ice time and the team captaincy, all in the name of acquiring the talent. For some players, the goal can be just making a AAA hockey team. For Mike, playing AAA hockey—the highest level for kids—was never in question. But being a AAA captain, that was pure prestige.

"At the time, we were playing for the Red Wings, the best team in the province. You don't want to leave the best team in the province but I wasn't happy about the way Mike was being used by the coach. My first impression of Frost was that he was kind of quiet, very sure of himself, and a little weird. There was something about him that was a little different, but I really didn't pay attention to that. He was relentless in coming after us. Frost continued to come to every game we played and he kept talking to me. He wasn't letting go of this."

When Mike Jefferson's AAA Red Wings team went on to win the Ontario provincial championship, it should have been a reason to celebrate. But Steve wasn't celebrating. He was too wrapped up in his own son's game to enjoy the team victory. "I was pissed because Mike didn't play a lot. I think he only got four shifts in the final game. I didn't take that kind of thing well. I was really mad. You know how fathers get about these things. They take it personally."

In the arena parking lot following the game, Steve was still steaming when David Frost appeared and started up the conversation that would change the Jeffersons' lives forever.

"Dave came up to me and said, 'Do you still want to play on this team?' It was clear he saw I was upset."

"If you come with me, I'll play your kid to death."

Steve thought for a moment and wanted more.

"Can he still wear the C?"

Frost said he'd already committed the captaincy to Sheldon Keefe. That was news to Steve, but in the cutthroat world of minor hockey, even good friends don't always share recruiting secrets. "He said I waited too long to commit. But by that time, Brian Keefe and I were very good friends. I couldn't begrudge Sheldon because we waited too long to give him an answer. Besides, I knew what kind of player and kid Sheldon was. We decided to go to Frost's team and Mike got an A for alternate captain on his jersey. We were excited by that. Sheldon the captain; Mike the alternate. And that's how it all began with Frost, at the age of twelve. It all started so good."

But right from the beginning, in the first game Mike Jefferson ever played for Frost, there should have been alarm bells of some kind for a parent. But Steve Jefferson missed all the signs. He was caught up in the circumstance.

His new team, the Young Nats, were playing in a tournament in Buffalo to begin the season and Steve was as excited about a new season as he had ever been and his chest was out. His son was wearing an A for a hard-nosed coach who bent over backwards to recruit him, getting the kind of opportunity he had been waiting for, struggling for.

What could be better than this?

Steve also saw his son motivated to play like he had never been before, showing a significant jump for the brief time he'd been training and working with Frost. Everything, it seemed, was working right, until Mike crashed into the boards, fell to the ice, and complained about feeling numb. It was probably twenty minutes before Mike Jefferson got to his feet and was helped from the ice. His father was frantic.

"You get very scared when something like that happens to your kid," said Steve. "You almost get panicky. And when I got to him, all the time he was telling me, 'Dad, dad, my back is killing me.'"

At least it wasn't the head, wasn't the neck, wasn't the kind of collision that could end a young boy's hockey career. But it was something and it seemed serious at the time. The arena nurse wrapped a blanket around Mike Jefferson in the dressing room. By that time, Steve was in the dressing room as well, a place where parents of players at that level of hockey are usually not allowed to be. "Are you going to be all right?" Steve asked his son.

He didn't get an immediate answer, which concerned him. At that point, Frost walked into the dressing room. "To be honest," said Steve. "I've never seen anything like it."

"What the fuck are you doing in here?!" Frost shouted, tearing into both father and son for being in the team dressing room while the game was still on.

"Mike," he fumed, "get that goddamned blanket off, there's a third period to play!"

"And like nothing even happened to him, Michael got up, threw off the blanket, and went back to the bench, ready to go. And I didn't know what to think. And I never said another word about it. Not to Dave. Not to Mike. Not really to anyone. I just let it go. I gave him that power over my son. I let him decide. I can't believe, looking back, that I did that. I just stood there saying nothing; I got caught up in the game.

"I'm a victim of chasing the dream."

The Dave Frost that Steve Jefferson wants to kill used to be his friend. Or, at least, he thought they were friends. It was all part of the illusion.

As time went on and the relationship built, Frost and Steve would spend hours on the phone, often late at night, usually talking hockey. If they weren't talking about Mike, they would be talking about the team, or the last game, or the next game. "The conversations seemed endless to me," said Sue Jefferson. "I didn't know what they were talking about, but they spent an awful lot of time on the phone. Some nights, they'd go to one or two in the morning talking on the phone. They were like girlfriends, with all that chatter."

If it wasn't on the phone, it was in person. And often Frost and Jefferson would watch hockey films together, and break down the play into minute details. Steve loved being an insider, thinking he was involved with decisions and important hockey matters.

"He wouldn't talk to any parent on the team but me," said Steve. "He hated most of the parents. After the game, he would phone me and we would talk from ten at night to one in the morning. Dave would talk to me about different parents, different kids. I was right in the middle of everything."

But as the relationship evolved, and as Steve believed he was growing closer to Frost, there was more reason for concern. He just wasn't able to see it all then. His son was pulling away, and Frost was moving in to fill the void. "To be honest, I had blinders on," said Steve.

It was only years later that Steve realized how cruelly he had been betrayed.

"One time, Mike played a pretty bad game. After the game, Frost came up to me and said, 'Give him shit on the way home. Tear into him.' Then he told me what I should say to Mike. So we got in the truck for the drive home and I lit into Mike. Just like Frost said. And then I learned later that Frost would go up to Mike and say something like, 'I bet your dad really gave you shit last night. I bet you he said this and this to you.' And then he'd say something derogatory about me. Mike thought he was some kind of wizard, that he knew everything. What we didn't know was how we were being played.

"Dave would get things on me and then use them against me. He'd find something out about me and he'd ask Mike something like, 'Did your father go to jail? Why'd your dad go to jail? Your dad is a drunk.' He'd find something out and then use it against me. 'You don't want to be like him. You don't want to go to jail.' Dave and I would talk on the phone for hours, and I would tell him things, but I didn't realize until afterwards that he was turning everything against me. The more he learned about me, the more he used against me. That just made him more powerful in Michael's eyes."

On the one hand, Frost would confide in Steve and make it

appear as though they were friends and close companions with the same goal in mind. But on the other hand, he was working hard at separating Mike from his family.

During his two-week nightmare at Frost's cottage, young Tom Jefferson saw first-hand how the man his father spent hours talking to on the phone would deride him when he wasn't around, how he would insult Steve Jefferson to exert influence over his sons. "Frost would refer to my dad as a worthless piece of shit or an alcoholic or a bum, and he'd say, 'You don't want to end up like him, do you? You're better than that,'" says Tom.

Tom managed to keep his distance and stay within the orbit of his family. But Mike was completely sucked in by Frost's manipulations. Some of the stories Mike came to believe are simply not true. There is no proof that the violent, non-loving upbringing that Mike talks about ever happened. Some of the stories that were drummed into his head, over and over again, were missing nuance or context or basic fact.

"Mike would tell people we had a violent house and that there were violent outbursts in the house," said Sue. "I've seen him reference that. He would talk about me getting hit. I can tell you, with absolute certainty, that Steve has never hit me. There was one story we told a lot that he completely misunderstood. One time, I was kind of playfully sparring with Steve and saying something like, 'You're not so tough, you're not so tough.' And I was bouncing around throwing fists like a boxer, very playfully. And then I hit him, probably harder than I wanted to, and he and the chair fell completely backwards. It was one of those crazy things that happen. He's lying on the chair on the ground, backwards, laughing his head off because I'd knocked him down and I'm jumping up and down like I'm champion of the world.

"We told that story a lot. But by the time it got to Dave and then back to us, it was about violence and us having a violent home. There was no violence to it at all. It was just play fighting."

When Dave Frost moved his family to within blocks of Steve and his family, the Jeffersons felt the effect on the fabric of their daily lives immediately. Whenever something went wrong at his own house, or he didn't get his way, Mike would go to Frost's place. And sometimes, when he got in trouble (as teenagers are apt to do), his first phone call wasn't to his parents.

At the age of thirteen, Mike Jefferson was arrested for the very first time. The charge was shoplifting, a typical crime for children of that age.

Mike's first phone call was not to his father or mother, but to Frost, who agreed to pick up Steve Jefferson and head to the department store where the alleged crime had been committed. When they all piled into Frost's car, Steve couldn't contain himself any longer.

"What the fuck is wrong with you?" he barked at his son, and punctuated his question with a smack. He then told Mike that he was kicked out of his house. He didn't mean it—it was a spur-of-the-moment threat, the kind any parent might make. But it may have been the biggest mistake of his life. Unlike most teenagers, Mike Jefferson actually had a place to go. A place he was quite comfortable with. For refuge, he went to Dave Frost's house.

And that became the trend. If he was faced with discipline, if the family had an argument—for almost any reason—Mike would leave his family home and walk to Frost's house. While Steve was concerned, he never thought it would be permanent. He thought it was the age, the time, just a phase. Mike was getting better as a hockey player, distancing himself from those he was playing with and against. "If he wasn't the best hockey player on every team he played on, he was second best," said Steve. "I knew a lot of kids around our neighbourhood, kids older than him, who had gone through some trouble, so I thought he'd be okay in the long term. I just let things happen. I let too much happen. Honest, I thought he'd grow out of this.

"I know Mike did a couple of cycles of steroids, if that's what you call it. I knew he did that and I never said anything about it. And I wonder what it did to his behaviour. He was trying to get there [the NHL] and that if it helped, who was I to ask about it? And my friends and people I knew kept telling me, 'Don't worry about him. He's going to grow out of this. You'll see, when he's eighteen or nineteen, he'll come home.' And I truly believed that would happen. It never happened. Or I guess it never happened until he tried to have Frost killed. I think I understand what he was doing. He was saying, 'This has gone on for too long. I want out.' But he didn't know how to get out."

As time went on, and more stories about Frost began to emerge after the estrangement of Mike from his family, Steve's frustration grew and his behaviour, at times, got more erratic. He thought he knew what was going on in his son's life. He believed he knew. In the teenage years, Mike's hockey development took precedence over anything else—as long as that was on the upswing, Steve didn't think he had anything to worry about.

All that changed, after the photographs were found from Tom's two weeks at Frost's cottage. The photographs were the most graphic evidence of Frost's abuse of Tom, and the Brampton boys' approval of it. They showed pictures of Tom being taped naked to a bed, and the series of abusive acts that first took him to speak to the police. The discovery of those photos was the final wedge that drove Mike away from his family, and divided the family like never before. And the more Mike and Frost separated themselves from the Jeffersons, the angrier Steve became.

And when the CBC aired the first hour of Bob McKeown's two-part, award-winning documentary on *the fifth estate*, well, Steve Jefferson just couldn't contain himself. It's one thing for a father to think he knows something. It's another to see his life, his son's life, and his family's life unfold before him in his own home, on his own TV. It wasn't just his story any more. It was a disturbing, revealing story that all of Canada could watch—and it was more than he could take. And he was in the middle of all of it.

At the end of the show, he dialled Frost's phone and he kept on dialling and leaving messages. Among them, "You sick fucking son of a bitch. You are sick."

"And I went on and on …

"I was kind of crazed when I heard that Mike said 'I love you' to him from prison. That just made me crazy. I'm calling his phone and saying, 'Dave, I love you. Dave, do you love me, Dave?' And I'd hang up and do it again."

Frost eventually called the police to complain. The police called Steve Jefferson and told him to stop harassing Frost. "They told me I had to stop harassing him or they were going to charge me.

"I told them that they know my prior history. Harassment is the least of my worries. But I told the cops I'd try and leave him alone."

Steve claims to have called Frost ten to fifteen times after *the fifth estate*'s hour-long program aired.

"I'd be saying things like, 'Dave, you're a faggot.' Or, 'Dave, you're a pedophile.' Or, 'Dave, you're a freak.' There was nothing I could do to this man to even up what he'd done to me. And when

I got up the next morning at 4:30, I walked into the bathroom and the first thing I saw was the cellphone. And I guess I couldn't help myself. So I phoned him again.

"I said, 'Frost, I still love you. Let's get together.' And I just went on and on. I must have been quite crazed about the whole thing."

That morning, Steve got a call from Tom Trevelyan, a Peel Regional Police officer he knew, who happened to be a former professional hockey player and also the dad of a future pro. "Steve," he said on the phone, "the OPP is coming to arrest you today."

"Can't I work through my lunch?" Steve asked, knowing something was coming.

"Don't think so," said Trevelyan.

Parked outside a local hospital at lunch hour were six police officers, who showed up to arrest Steve Jefferson. "I don't know why they needed six guys. I would have surrendered myself to them. And as I'm getting arrested, I was worried because I was supposed to be on the Bill Watters radio show at noon that day, talking about the *fifth estate* show."

The police bundled Steve into a waiting vehicle and set out on the two-hour drive to Belleville, the closest jurisdiction to Kingston, where Frost was then living. On his way to be finger-printed and officially charged with harassment, the police in the car were listening to what was then called MOJO Radio with Bill Watters and Jeff Marek hosting in the early afternoon. Steve asked if he could call his brother so he could let the radio hosts know he wouldn't be available that day, and the cops complied. Soon, he got confirmation that the message had got through.

"While in the squad car, I heard Bill Watters say that I'd be on the show later on and then he said a few minutes afterward that I won't be available for the show today because I had been arrested."

The radio station had its scoop. Steve Jefferson had his handcuffs and was soon to be booked and fingerprinted for harassment—yet another arrest in a life with too many of them.

August 1, 2006

Dear Mike

It's been awhile since my last letter to you. I find it hard to find something new to say. It would be easier if we could write each other, then there would be something to write back and forth about.

I have found out through a good friend of yours that you are enjoying writing poems and songs. This makes me smile. I'm happy that you have an outlet to put your feelings into. This is good.

Mike, you don't have to keep silent anymore. No one will ever believe any of Dave's bullshit anyway. He has lied to so many people that his breath smells.

Please find it in yourself to open up. Let's put the right person in prison. Free yourself. We are all here to help you. I have open arms for you. So does your Dad and Tom and don't forget Grandma and Grandpa, and you know everyone else. This is a long list of your real family waiting for you. We are all willing to help in any way.

Please don't turn your back when you need to lean on someone. Your family is here for you to lean on. That's what family is all about. Being there when you need them. We are here and you know what? We need you.

So why not lean on each other. It might help.

Please write me.

Love you

Mom

[This letter was returned with the following words on the front of the envelope: "Go Fuck Yourself," "Return to Sender," and "No Jefferson Danton." The following was on the back of the envelope: "Stop Writing," "Go fuck yourself," and "Your wasting Your time."]

"The Most Powerful Man in Hockey"

As a young Mike Jefferson began to develop as a minor-hockey player worth watching, a Michigan lawyer named Bob Goodenow was emerging as the most feared and powerful man in all of professional hockey.

These two people couldn't have been more opposite. On the one hand, there was the former captain of the Harvard hockey team and then executive director of the National Hockey League Players' Association, a domineering browbeater capable of going toe-to-toe against the collective might of the NHL's owners. On the other there was Jefferson, the dead-end kid who claims to have grown up in squalor, scratching and clawing his way up the hockey ladder. But for nearly a decade and through gales of controversy, their lives remained entwined in ways impossible to untangle. While they may have been from different worlds and income brackets so far apart they needed maps to find each other, their paths somehow kept crossing.

It is difficult to accurately measure influence. No one can know exactly what would have happened if this or that person hadn't come into the life of another. No one can say that Mike Danton's life would have turned out better if Bob Goodenow had not been part of it—for all anyone knows, it could have turned out worse. However, one thing is certain: it would have turned out very differently. Though the influence of the head of the NHLPA would be subtle, it would also be profound.

Goodenow was in St. Louis in the days before Danton's botched murder-for-hire attempt. In fact, he had dinner with Danton while he was in town. What they talked about is unknown, but they must have had plenty of fodder for conversation, since Goodenow had known Danton since he was little Mike Jefferson playing minor hockey in Toronto. Goodenow had been part of Danton's life for years, and had played a role in nearly every step of the hockey player's career. Goodenow had been behind the bench, telling Danton what to do on the ice; he'd helped determine where Danton played, how Danton played, even who represented Danton as an agent when the time came to think about making the jump to pro.

There is no doubt about it. Goodenow had helped Danton along over the years. The scrappy kid from the suburbs must have been grateful for the involvement in his career of one of the biggest personalities in the game. But then, minor hockey makes strange bedfellows. The connection between Jefferson and Goodenow?

David Frost.

"You want to hear something stupid? I actually introduced Bob Goodenow to Dave Frost," says Steve Jefferson, laughing uncomfortably at the sad irony of his words. He is sitting at the kitchen table of his home in Erin, telling minor-hockey story after minor-hockey story—all of them detailed, so many involving Goodenow, or Frost, or both, as if they happened yesterday.

It was 1993, and Frost was still trying to recruit Mike Jefferson away from the Red Wings. He was calling and showing up at games. Then one day, he happened to call Steve Jefferson while Steve was talking to the NHLPA executive. "We were at Chesswood Arena with the Red Wings and Frost called me on my cellphone and said, 'Tell these guys I'll coach them.'"

"Who are you talking to?" Goodenow asked.

When Jefferson told Goodenow he was talking to a guy named David Frost, who wanted to coach the team, the man who would very soon be taking over the NHLPA said, "Who does this piece of shit think he is?"

Goodenow was looking for a minor-hockey coach and was dead set against Frost, whom he knew nothing about. Frost went on to coach the Toronto Young Nationals minor-hockey team, rather than the Wings, but Goodenow observed him from up close while his son played for the Wings.

It wasn't until Goodenow found out that Frost's fiancée (later his wife) was Bridget McCauley, daughter of the highly respected former NHL director of officiating John McCauley, that he began to change his mind. The McCauley name gave Frost a halo of respectability he would not otherwise have enjoyed. "Once Bob found out about Bridget, he changed his mind completely about Frost," said Jefferson. "It was like, if he's connected to John McCauley, he must be okay. Like that gave him some kind of credibility and approval." What Goodenow didn't know then was that the McCauley family, the father having passed away, the mother Irene in tears on a daily basis, was almost completely estranged from their daughter, who had left home as a teenager to be with Frost. And the well-known hockey family that so impressed Goodenow wanted nothing to do with Frost. They just hoped Bridget would come home.

But Frost's relationship with his in-laws mattered less and less to Goodenow as his unlikely bond with Frost grew deeper. If Frost wasn't going to coach the Red Wings, then Joey Goodenow would have to move to the Nats. And that is just what happened.

"Within a year or so after they first met, you wouldn't hear a bad word about Frost coming from Bob. He was his greatest advocate. Frost was the coach [of the Young Nats] and Bob over time became his unofficial assistant. And you have to understand something about the politics of this. You had to listen to Bob because of who he is. He had this aura about him. He's an intimidating man. Bob was never my friend, and I was never his friend, but he had this way of keeping you in line. You didn't second-guess Bob. You did what he said.

"And always he was placating me, always giving me hockey tickets to Leafs games or other things I guess, because he wanted Mike to play with his son, Joey, and he knew what Frost thought of Mike. I got a lot of Leafs tickets in those days; it made me feel like a big shot almost. Bob would do funny things to impress you. One time, we were at a tournament in Lindsay, Ontario, and I walked up to Bob's car in the parking lot and he was on the phone. He rolled down the window and handed me the cellphone and said there was somebody who wanted to talk to me.

"It was Brett Hull on the phone. And here I am having this conversation with Brett Hull and Brett's saying, 'I've heard a lot about you.' And I'm thinking to myself, 'Like hell you have'—but that's the way Goodenow did things. You would feel good because you talked to Brett Hull. Like that mattered, like it was going to change your life or something. If he needed you for something, you were his buddy and he'd make you feel special.

"If he didn't need you, you were nothing."

That Young Nats team won an Ontario hockey championship. Mike Jefferson and Joey Goodenow played together—they were coached by Frost, with Bob Goodenow's assistance. And Steve Jefferson was in the role he enjoyed most: lead parent. Not that Frost went easy on any kids, even Goodenow's.

At one point over the course of that 1995–96 season, Frost was reported to have taken a dressing-room garbage can full of trash and dumped it on Joey Goodenow's head. "If you're going to play like garbage," he is reported to have said, "you're going to look like garbage."

Goodenow, the father, has always denied that the garbage-can incident ever happened, but many eyewitnesses claim it to be true. He has claimed that he never saw Frost abuse any players, including son Joe and Mike Jefferson (it's worth noting here that Goodenow senior turned down interview requests for this book).

But perhaps Goodenow's thoughts on parenting may differ from the views of other fathers. According to Steve, Joey did not like driving home with his father after games. Apparently, Goodenow could be quite harsh in his post-game assessment and this was uncomfortable for the young player.

"There were games when Mike would come to me and say, 'Can we give Joey a lift home? He doesn't want to go home with his dad.'

"I didn't want to do it. I didn't want to get between Goodenow and his son," says Steve Jefferson.

It wasn't just Steve Jefferson who was reluctant to cross swords with Bob Goodenow. Mike Futa, a former junior-hockey coach and general manager and currently the co-director of amateur scouting for the Los Angeles Kings, was introduced early in his professional career to the Goodenow–Frost connection. In 1996, before Frost, Mike Jefferson, Sheldon Keefe, and company wound up with the Quinte Hawks, a pitch had been made for them to play tier-two junior hockey for the St. Michael's Buzzers. Futa was the head coach of that team, playing out of the arena at the history-laden Toronto school St. Michael's College.

"I remember having a meeting with Bob Goodenow and another father, Don Batten, about having their kids [and others] come to play for St. Mike's. Some of the kids were already going to the school. Goodenow wanted all the kids [from the provincial champion Young Nats] to play together. So on the one hand, I'm trying to sell him and all the players on the program. On the other hand, I inferred from Bob, really more than inferred, that he could deliver all those kids to me if I was willing to bring in Dave Frost as my assistant coach. I knew a little about Frost by reputation from my own playing days. He was kind of small potatoes at the time, but he still had something of a reputation around hockey—and it wasn't a good one.

"I thought about it really hard. I was just starting my coaching career. These kids could really have helped me. But after thinking about it and thinking about it, there was really no chance I could make that deal with Bob. The players would have helped us a lot, but I couldn't have Dave Frost as my assistant coach at St. Mike's, where the school motto is *Goodness, Discipline, Knowledge*. Even back then, with Frost's reputation, that wouldn't have passed the smell test.

"But what I do remember from that meeting was feeling a little intimidated. I think everybody did when they met Bob Goodenow. He was authoritarian. When he spoke, the room would go quiet.

Bob Goodenow swore by Frost as a coach. He said the guy was doing unbelievable things with these kids."

And just like Steve Jefferson, Goodenow, too, was caught up in the success his own son, Joey, was having.

"But, think of it from my perspective, as a young guy just starting out as a coach," says Futa. "It was pretty easy to be intimidated by Goodenow. He had a huge presence. Like nothing I'd ever experienced before. You could see why he was capable of doing what he did. If he said something, you listened to it because he was Bob Goodenow.

"And all the while, I'm thinking, 'Here's the most powerful man in hockey and he's giving his blessing to Dave Frost as being an unbelievable mentor for these kids.' That's something I had to listen to. It wasn't easy for me to say no."

The players, for a while, did stay together, moving as a group to the Bramalea Blues of the Ontario Provincial Junior Hockey League. But even that didn't last long. Within ten games, Frost had corralled Jefferson, Keefe, Shawn Cation, Darryl Tiveron, and Larry Barron and moved them to the Quinte Hawks of the outlaw Metro Junior Hockey League. The only one of the group who remained in Bramalea: Joey Goodenow.

Joey Goodenow might not have been going over the boards for David Frost any more, but by no means did that mean that his father had had a falling out with his coach. Far from it. Years later, when some of Frost's players were suiting up for the St. Michael's Majors in the Ontario Hockey League, they would play regular Saturday afternoon games before small crowds at Maple Leaf Gardens. In one corner of the arena, almost always by themselves, Frost and Goodenow would sit and watch the games together. Often, Steve Jefferson said, they would watch hockey films and break them down together. As unusual as it seemed, Frost, who often looked like he'd just rolled out of a gutter, and Goodenow, the businesslike millionaire-maker, spent an inordinate amount of time together. Goodenow became something of a professional advocate for Frost, pushing hockey teams to hire him, trying to convince NHL executives he was an up-and-coming hockey coach.

Why was Goodenow, a man so extreme and difficult that the National Hockey League essentially shut down its league for a year in order to have him removed from the NHLPA, unflappably interested in someone like Frost? The time they spent coaching together can't possibly explain the extraordinary intimacy of their relationship or the steadfastness of Goodenow's advocacy. This bond lasted from Goodenow's time as a minor-hockey assistant coach in 1993 right up until the last, chaotic days of Danton's NHL career and beyond that, even. It's not a coincidence in any way that in the recorded prison conversations between Danton and Frost, Frost makes numerous references to having support from "the man." "The man" quite clearly was Goodenow.

When the time came for Mike Jefferson to pick a player agent, the two most influential people involved in the selection were not Steve and Sue Jefferson. Usually, the selection comes down to parents and son putting their heads together and doing what feels right. Only by this time, around 1997, Mike's parents were all but out of the picture. The decision in this case would be made by Frost and Goodenow. And the decision, in retrospect, was pretty obvious.

By 1997, Frost had already begun doing unofficial bird-dog work for the player agent Mike Gillis, a former NHL player and the current general manager of the 2010–11 Stanley Cup finalist

Vancouver Canucks, who worked out of Kingston, Ontario. Being a bird dog means travelling to many arenas, watching young men play, and trying to find the appropriate level of talent to turn over to the agent to represent for the future.

Frost was essentially a hockey middle man for Gillis. All the major agents have bird dogs working for them across Canada, the United States, and Europe—it's how they find and develop their client base.

So it was obvious that Frost would turn his boys, including Mike Jefferson, over to Gillis for representation.

"As a father, I don't even know who Mike Gillis was or how he wound up as Mike's agent," said Steve Jefferson, rather sheepishly. "I wish I could tell you the details. This is the kind of thing a father and son are supposed to know, supposed to do together. But by the time Mike needed an agent, pretty much everything was out of our hands. Dave was looking after all the hockey decisions. He made that clear to us. Mike made it clear. If we tried to get involved, he'd shut us out or Mike would shut us out or they would threaten to. So what choice did we have? We could get involved and chance losing our son or stay in the background and hope for the best.

"The way I've come to understand the arrangement over time, Bob Goodenow basically set the whole thing up. He got Dave to work for Gillis. And Frost got Gillis to represent Mike and some of the other boys."

The Gillis–Goodenow connection was not anything new. Unlike Goodenow, who tried to make it in professional hockey as a player, Gillis was supposed to be a big-time player. He was a high NHL draft pick who turned out to be a bust of a player. Goodenow wasn't expected to make the NHL; Gillis, drafted fifth overall in 1978 by the Colorado Rockies, was expected to become a star.

But after fizzling out as a player—his career ended due to injury—he went to law school and, after being called to the bar, he went to war with the hockey establishment. Gillis's now famous victory in a Toronto court over his former agent, Alan Eagleson, played a large role in leading to Eagleson's removal as head of the NHL Players' Association. With Eagleson out as executive director of the NHLPA, the new man for the job just happened to be Goodenow, who at the time was a player agent in partnership with a fellow Harvard graduate named Brian Burke.

Over time, Gillis became a prominent player agent, representing such stars as Pavel Bure and Markus Naslund, who played their best seasons for the Vancouver Canucks. But before that, he counted more on the help of friends like Goodenow. Agents need clients, players need agents, and Goodenow was the point at which the careers of Mike Danton, Mike Gillis and David Frost intersected.

Gillis didn't understand what all the fuss was about regarding Frost back in 1999. "Take a look at Sheldon Keefe," said Gillis. "He's an 80-plus student. It's his first year [in the OHL]. He'll finish with 50 goals and 125 points. The kid is an example we should be holding up of what we want in the OHL."

Gillis, today in his executive position of power and influence with the Canucks, has distanced himself from Frost over the years. But the confident optimism he expressed in 1999 allowed him to leave his bird dog in control of the day-to-day lives of his clients. When Danton was fighting his way into the NHL, it was Frost, not Gillis, who was left to shepherd the young player.

While Goodenow has spoken publicly on occasion about his relationship with Frost, Gillis has tried to bury this part of his past, contradicting himself on occasion and changing the story as it suited his needs. Like Goodenow, he refused to be interviewed for this book—his way of distancing himself from any connection to David Frost or the Jeffersons.

"I've talked to Mike about this," said Lou Lamoriello, general manager of the New Jersey Devils. "I think Mike [Gillis] is one of the few people who did right by Jefferson. I don't think he's a bad guy in any of this. I think he got into a situation he didn't want to be in, and once he saw what was happening, he didn't want any part of it any more."

When the photographs of the abuse of Tom Jefferson were discovered in 2002, Steve and Sue tried to deal with their latest family tumult as best they could. They called Goodenow. He called Dr. Brian Shaw of the NHL Players' Association. Shaw called the Children's Aid Society. All the Jeffersons were looking for was help and advice. They also called a surprised Mike Gillis.

"I called Gillis and I asked him, 'What the hell is going on here?'" Steve Jefferson remembers.

"Then he got on me. He said, 'What's taken you so long to call me? I've never had two players [Sheldon Keefe being the other] where the parents were so distant.' I wanted to know where he was and he wanted to know where I was. And then he said, 'I have nothing to do with David Frost.... You should have come to me a long time ago.'"

Not long after his only conversation with Steve Jefferson, Gillis resigned as agent of record for Mike Danton. "I think he more or less washed his hands of the whole thing," said Steve.

When Mike Gillis washed his hands of Mike Danton in 2002, he was putting the young man directly into the hands of the guy who used to work for him: David Frost.

By 2002, the small-time minor-hockey coach and Svengali had become certified as a professional player agent. Even Frost's eventual agent certification was pushed through by executive director Goodenow, which was unusual by NHLPA standards—especially in the case of a candidate with a rap sheet that included assault, suspensions from entire leagues, and forgery. Questions were asked, but according to a former high-end executive of the NHLPA, if Goodenow wanted Frost certified as a player agent, he was going to get certified. That's just the way things worked.

"One day, and I can't remember the date, Bob walked into Ian Penny's office and said, 'You'll certify David Frost,'" the former executive says, not wanting his name revealed. "Ian Penny (who was later ousted as interim executive director of the NHLPA long after Goodenow was fired) was the associate counsel at the time. He just did what he was told to do and didn't question it at all. Later, when some of us had questions, when the stories started to come out about Frost, and it was making us look bad, you'd never get an answer. If people asked Bob about it, he would basically ignore the question or treat them with disdain. That happened a few times to a few people. After a while, because of that, you stopped asking."

Said Steve Jefferson, "Goodenow's steadfast support of Frost was difficult to challenge. Typical of Bob, he wouldn't hear of any kind of challenge."

With Frost certified as a player agent, it was through Goodenow's will that he pushed others to see if they would leave their agents and join up with Frost. Brett Hull denies he was asked to sign on with Frost after his agent, Mike Barnett, became an NHL executive, but others insist that to be true.

After midnight on April 16, 2004, Steve Jefferson picked up the phone and called Bob Goodenow.

Earlier that night, he was in his usual perch, in the living room, watching hockey. The Ottawa Senators beat the Leafs 4–1 to knot their first-round playoff series at two games apiece. After the game, CBC's *The National* came on. The lead story that night: Mike Danton had been arrested in San Jose in the botched murder-for-hire plot.

With his heart racing and pounding, his face red and his body shaking, Steve could think of nothing but the hope that Goodenow might shed some light on a situation that had, impossibly, gone from horrific to even worse. He dialled and dialled and the phone rang and rang. "I would call him over and over again," said Steve. "But I couldn't contact him."

This went on for days. Steve Jefferson would call and there would be no response. "After a while, the whole thing was making me a little crazy. You have to understand. My son was arrested. And the one person who I thought could help him wouldn't take my calls."

Then, after several days of trying, Steve got a call from Goodenow's lawyer. "Bob has asked me to speak with you on his behalf," said the unfamiliar voice.

The one time Steve really needed Goodenow's help, he was nowhere to be found.

"I don't give a fuck who you are," Steve shouted. "I don't want to talk to you. You tell Bob I want to talk to him."

What Steve Jefferson didn't know at the time was that just a few nights before Mike was arrested in San Jose for attempting the hit on Frost, Goodenow had been out for dinner in St. Louis with Danton and Frost after Game 2 of the Sharks–Blues series. He had also been to the Blues' home playoff games against the Sharks, seated in the press box beside Frost.

"I never knew who Frost was," said Larry Pleau, then general manager of the Blues. "Certainly, I'd read about him and heard about him, and everybody kind of knew the stories that had been around, but I didn't know what he looked like. The first time I ever saw him was in the press box that night when I asked somebody, 'Who's that with Bob?'"

That very morning, Mike Danton was trying to arrange Frost's death on the telephone. Four days later, Danton was in prison. Yet it took almost two weeks for Goodenow to personally contact Steve Jefferson.

"Hey Steve," he called one day out of the blue, sounding casual and, as always, in control. "What's going on?"

"You tell me what's going on," said Steve.

Jefferson had tried for days to get to Goodenow, a powerful man, a voice of reason, someone he thought he could get an answer from or at least some advice. Their conversation didn't get very far. Goodenow offered no help of any kind. "We'll have to let the legal system take care of this and the truth will come out," Jefferson remembers Goodenow saying.

Steve Jefferson hung up the phone frustrated. After a decade of being placated by Goodenow, showered with tickets, that was it. Years earlier, when Goodenow wanted a coaching change at the minor-hockey level so he could return to a position of influence himself, he crafted a letter supposedly written by the parents on the Toronto Red Wings' minor-hockey team. He wrote the letter, complaining about the man coaching their team, indicating the parents were fed up and wanted change. The letter was unsigned. The first parent he took the letter to was Steve Jefferson.

"I signed the bloody thing and I didn't even agree with it," said Steve. "I did it because Bob Goodenow gave it to me to sign. That's the way things worked with Bob. He used his influence whenever and wherever he could. And he knew once I signed the letter, everybody else would sign. That's the way it worked around him. Everybody else signed it. We got rid of the coach. And Goodenow and his buddy were again in charge of the team.

"The truth in all this, Goodenow is an asshole. He got along with me because he knew I would be the voice to the parents. He used me. And when I needed him, where was he?"

Steve Jefferson thought about that, how he had gone to bat for Goodenow, and when he needed Goodenow's help the most, it was nowhere to be found. That disingenuous phone call in 2004, after Mike's arrest, was the last time they would ever speak.

The late Bill Wirtz, owner of the Chicago Blackhawks, was considered a backwards operator in almost all facets of the modern hockey world. For some reason, though, Wirtz took great personal interest in the Mike Danton–David Frost murder-for-hire story. He didn't know either man. But as someone deeply involved with the development of minor hockey in Illinois, he wanted to understand what few cared to ask about. He wanted to know how the Danton–Frost relationship came to be, and what part the NHL and NHLPA played in facilitating that relationship.

The year before his death, Wirtz sent a letter, dated August 23, 2006, addressed to Ted Saskin, then executive director of the NHLPA (Goodenow's short-lived successor) and copied to NHL commissioner Gary Bettman and his deputy, Bill Daly. In the letter, Wirtz, the former chair of the NHL's board of governors, called the

Danton–Frost incident "the worst event that I have experienced in fifty years associated with the NHL."

Wirtz went on in the letter to blame Goodenow for Frost's certification as a player agent, which enabled him to be ultra-involved in the lives of those players he had already controlled. "Right from the get-go this incident had great potential to damage the NHL," Wirtz wrote to Saskin, Bettman, and Daly. "Mr. Goodenow said he did not think so and continued to certify him (Frost) as an agent representing young hockey players ...

"The NHL's hands were tied from giving us further help because they were engaged in collective bargaining with the NHLPA, who insisted that David Frost was certified after a thorough investigation by your Association as well as your special committee. Who reviews these applications?

"Would you please send me the names and addresses of the gentlemen who served on the agent certification committee? ...

"In short, I am appalled by the handing of this time bomb. We all know the inappropriate handling of this matter is Bob Goodenow, who is counting his $8 million (having been pushed out of the PA) in Florida."

Wirtz followed up his letter to Saskin, Bettman, and Daly with a letter to the *Toronto Sun* dated September 13, 2006. Wirtz wrote that "on numerous occasions I asked Bob [Goodenow] to temporarily suspend David Frost's certification until after the Ontario Provincial Police had concluded their criminal investigation of him. Needless to say, he did nothing. By his lack of action in this matter, it certainly convinced me there is more to his certification matter than has been printed. Eventually the whole story will come out and it will not be pretty."

Wirtz also wrote that NHL commissioner Bettman "could not

get involved with Frost's certification because he was negotiating a new CBA [collective bargaining agreement] at the time" and that had to take precedence over anything else he was involved with.

"I don't know if we'll ever get to the bottom of this," Wirtz wrote the *Sun*. "But Bob Goodenow's name is written all over this."

How much is Goodenow, and by extension the NHLPA, to blame for the mess that turned out to be Mike Danton's life?

We do know this much: From the time they first began coaching together, Goodenow was an unabashed advocate of Frost. He pushed him on to junior teams. He pushed some NHL teams to hire him as a developmental coach. He promoted Frost wherever possible. And even after he was aware of the terribly troubling Tom Jefferson photos from Frost's cottage, and the eventual involvement of NHLPA psychologist Brian Shaw, he still went ahead with Frost's agent certification and maintained their relationship and, it seems, their friendship.

When the matter of Frost was brought up, no matter who brought it to his attention, whether it was a media person or a concerned but uninvolved player agent, it was quickly ignored or dispatched elsewhere. And after a while, people—mostly media members—stopped asking questions.

Long after the disturbing photographs of Tom Jefferson were found, after Frost had been investigated—not once, but twice—by the OPP, his relationship with Goodenow remained intact. Frost could count on Goodenow's support right to the end of Mike Danton's brief NHL career, and well beyond. After the arrest, taped conversations from prison confirmed that Goodenow was on side with Danton and Frost, supposedly working for both the NHLPA member who was in prison and the NHLPA-certified agent he had attempted to kill. Goodenow had arranged for Brian Shaw to assess Danton in prison. And it was clear from Danton's taped conversations with Frost from inside prison that they were expecting the good doctor to act on their behalf.

"I saw nothing inappropriate or unusual either with Mike or between Mike and Dave," Goodenow told *The Globe and Mail* in 2004 of their St. Louis dinner. They talked about the usual things over dinner, mostly hockey matters.

Sue Jefferson, though, holds Goodenow responsible for being party to what she sees as Frost's long-term kidnapping of her son. She admits she does not understand the connection, but believes that "Dave has something on Bob." What she knows is that Goodenow is one of the few people who had a chance to make a difference in Mike's life and failed.

"He was one of the people who probably was strong enough to do something about it. He knew [about Frost's regime of control over his players], they all knew, and nobody would stand up and do the right thing. Nobody would do anything about it at all."

"I blame him a lot," said Steve Jefferson, who accepts his own share of culpability for his fractured family. "You go back and ask yourself questions. What happens if the NHLPA doesn't certify Dave Frost? Is it possible a credible agent—not Dave—gets hold of Mike? Maybe a credible agent, a real professional, could have changed everything. Mike needed somebody he could trust. He needed help and support. And with Bob, there was this stamp of approval regarding Frost when nobody else would do that for him. And that led to his certification and other things. With the kind of support Bob had for Frost, it was difficult for anyone to challenge that. Because if you were challenging Frost, you were challenging Goodenow.

"And who was I to be challenging the most powerful man in hockey?"

On his Sports Business News website, Howard Bloom was astonished by what Goodenow got away with.

"David Frost serves as a testament as to what's wrong with those who are ill-equipped to be coaching youngsters. By all appearances, David Frost was a self-serving, egomaniacal, borderline psychopath. How and why an individual of Frost's ilk ever became an NHL agent is an embarrassment to the National Hockey League Players' Association.... At the same time, someone should be held accountable within the NHLPA for allowing Dave Frost to be certified as an NHL player agent."

David Conte, the assistant general manager and director of scouting for the New Jersey Devils, who drafted Danton and in some ways befriended him, believes that almost everyone who came into contact with Mike Danton in a meaningful way let him down. That means his mom, his dad, Frost, and other friends and coaches. But he places Goodenow high on the long list of those to blame.

August 9, 2006

Mike

Hey I thought I'd write you a letter because I have not yet
done so. I just wanted to know what is going on with you and to
let you know how things are going for me. You may or may not
choose to write back but that is completely up to you. Right now
I am in Minnesota attending Minnesota Hockey Camps. It's run
by the San Jose Sharks—it's quite the development program.

Day three and my legs are holding up pretty good. I'm here
for two weeks to help prepare myself for my own camp on the 28th
of this month. This season, I'm trying out for the Barrie Colts,
after being sent down to Jr. A by the Oshawa Generals, because
I was told that I need to gain more confidence with the puck.
I finished last season playing with the Mississauga Chargers
and skating with the Ice Dogs. I picked up a total of, I think, 28
points in 35 games or so. I'm not proud of it but I am trying to
keep a positive head. Barrie's GM told me that they have a spot
for me, I just have to earn it. With this letter I've attached the
gym workout I've been doing, not including dry-land. If all
possible, maybe you could add or change and give me advice about
this program and the upcoming season whether it be positive or
negative. Whatever you feel necessary, to write.

I'm really hoping to hear back from you because you are my
brother and you are my idol. I have always looked up to you no
matter what the situation is. I've been told we look a lot alike
on and off the ice but I'm left-handed. Enough of the shit. I
want to hear back from you so that I can send you some tapes and
pictures of myself. Until the next time we speak or meet again,
just remember, I am your brother and I'm not going away.

Love you buddy,

Tom

8

Junior Daze

Mike Futa has a confession: he loved coaching Mike Jefferson in junior hockey.

Futa was the youngest coach in the Ontario Hockey League, trying to make a name for himself, and what he admired so much about Jefferson was his dedication, his commitment, his passion to play the game. It wasn't just Jefferson he admired. He also loved working with Sheldon Keefe on the Toronto St. Michael's Majors, the parent team of the tier-two St. Michael's Buzzers, in 1998–99.

To this day, Futa, long removed from the coaching world in his position as co-director of amateur scouting for the Los Angeles Kings, likes to refer to Jefferson as "my favourite player I've ever coached."

"There were so many things to like about Mike. He wasn't a problem in school. He outworked everybody on the ice in practice. He did the same in games. He was a bright kid with a nice personality. As a coach, Sheldon Keefe and Mike Jefferson were the two hardest-working kids I've ever been around."

That was the good part. Not everything else was good.

Jefferson was the first of the Dave Frost players to arrive with the Majors. Within a year, the four Brampton boys—Jefferson, Keefe, Shawn Cation, and Ryan Barnes—would be four of the best players on Futa's struggling St. Michael's team. With the new players on hand, the struggle wasn't so much with improving wins and losses, but with Futa's attempts at controlling the environment. He loved coaching Jefferson, the individual; he didn't love what he faced peripherally by coaching him.

"It didn't take me long to realize these were talented kids, the best players on my hockey team, and they were completely under the guidelines of someone else's direction," said Futa. They weren't listening to him; they were being guided by Frost.

"On the one side, you wanted that kind of player. On the other, you couldn't have that kind of team. It was complicated and frustrating. As a young coach, I knew I was failing miserably at how I was handling this. I loved the kids. I respected [Frost's] knowledge of the game. But I couldn't stand the way it was being communicated to me or to them. And it was undermining the whole concept of team. I'm trying to coach the team, and inside I know it's not working.

"I used to watch them do things and it was clear [Frost] knew his stuff. He would call audibles in the game and all of a sudden, whatever we were trying to do as a team, they were doing something different, often better. Jefferson would look directly up in the crowd. It was so obvious to anyone watching. Then all of a sudden there would be a switch or something and the puck would be in the net. I used to laugh to myself, 'That was pretty good, Dave.' It's an absolute shame, if you think back about it, because there was a pretty good hockey mind lost because of his personality and pretty good hockey players all under his command."

If St. Michael's had been winning games, perhaps Jefferson and friends would never have played for Mike Futa, and David Frost would not have had the chance to initiate his plan to get his boys all playing together on the Majors. But the guys on Futa's roster weren't getting the job done. Changes were inevitable. Management had to do something to get the right pieces in place. The Majors needed both skill and toughness and Frost convinced them he had those pieces in hand. So Frost began to manipulate the lives of kids playing in other places. And one by one, Frost orchestrated deals that moved his players to Toronto.

Jefferson began his OHL career in 1997–98 with Sarnia, but that lasted just twelve games before the team wanted no part of Frost's antics any more. Sarnia traded Jefferson to Toronto.

Sheldon Keefe was drafted by the OHL's Plymouth Whalers franchise in Michigan, but he didn't report to camp and told their organizers there that he was headed to Northern Michigan University on a hockey scholarship. He never went to the States and was eventually dealt by Plymouth to Toronto. Cation was selected by the Oshawa Generals, but from the beginning informed them he would never play there. They had no choice but to move him.

Frost had begun his remaking of the St. Mike's team, putting three of his Brampton boys together on one squad, in a location close enough to home that he could monitor all the activities.

"It was kind of strange how it all worked out," said Futa. "I remember when Frost approached us about doing this. He said, 'You can really put some pieces together if you do all of this.' He's talking about Sheldon with us and we're trying to work out a deal with Peter DeBoer in Plymouth and Frost says, 'If you get Sheldon's rights, he'll report here rather than go to college.' We made the trade and within an hour, Sheldon was there. I think he was told to wait in the parking lot, knowing the trade was going to be made. That doesn't happen often that you make a trade and the kid is there within minutes."

The change in players was supposed to change the fortunes of the St. Michael's junior team.

"Our whole dynamic changed," said Futa. "I eventually got pretty concerned about it. It was not talked about widely outside of our office, but we knew something was wrong. I didn't like what I was seeing, behaviour-wise. I liked the hockey part, but we didn't have a team. The four guys became their own team and all it did was divide us. I would worry about a kid like Mike Jefferson because really he was so dedicated to Frost, but I thought he was a great kid, and I'd see his father at everything. So I thought if his father is there, what do I have to worry about?

"That's the part I always wondered about. His dad never missed a thing. He was at every game, everything we had going on. His kid was playing thirty minutes or close to that a game. He's playing with his friends. He's one of our top scorers. Isn't that what it is supposed to be?

"Dave [Frost] was in heaven and, to be honest, Mr. Jefferson seemed to be loving it."

Frost and Steve Jefferson may have been loving the time with the St. Michael's Majors, but Futa and his bosses, Mark Napier and Reg Quinn, were not. They weren't winning games and internally there were all kinds of issues. Also unhappy was a player agent by the name of Darren Ferris, who still works for Bobby Orr's agency. Ferris's client, Charlie Stephens, was the first pick in the OHL Priority Draft in 1997, and was considered by many to be a star of the future. It was Ferris's job to protect Stephens's interests. The Majors believed they would build their team around Stephens's talents.

But as a former tier-two junior coach himself, Ferris was well aware of who Dave Frost was long before he was anything resembling a public figure. In fact, when the Majors began acquiring the Frost players, Ferris called Napier and Futa and warned them that they had "made a deal with the devil."

"Mike Futa thought I was off my rocker when I told him this," said Ferris. "They thought they had the situation in control. They thought they had an understanding with Frost that he wouldn't interfere. But I knew what he was all about from tier-two hockey. I was around for all the brawling and the targeting of kids. I heard a lot of the stories about kids living in his house and him promising kids, 'If you come with me, I'll get you to the NHL.' That was his sell. He always wanted the kids to leave home. I took a dislike to him instantly.

"And at the same time, I had to protect Charlie Stephens's interests. If you had a kid with that kind of promise, it was my job to do that. I didn't want him around that team. I didn't think it would be good for him and he didn't want to be there either. I was being proactive."

Early in his second season with the Majors, Stephens was traded to Sudbury and then to Guelph in a deal that brought Ryan Barnes to the Majors. That meant the four Brampton boys were together on the same team—just what Frost wanted, and what Futa thought he wanted. Everyone, including Ferris, was happy with the moves. Only it didn't work out the way the Majors had hoped. The Brampton boys were a four-man team, a unit unto themselves.

"As much as I liked and respected the kids, I knew they weren't listening to me," said Futa. "I was the coach, but someone else was coaching them. I would look out at the ice and I would love to say that was my power play or my faceoff play. But it was clear they were being coached by Dave. I'd see something on the ice and think, 'Where'd that come from?' And then I'd take a second and I knew.

"And every day, I'd be getting calls from Frost. Or pager messages … I don't think there were texts back then. Dave would say do this, or push these buttons, or you have to do that. To be honest, I respected his view of the game even if I didn't necessarily respect him."

From the very beginning, coaching the four Brampton boys was a challenge. Futa had a team to coach, but he didn't really have a team. He had a group of players divided.

"Their concept of team was how did it affect the four of them. Not the other eighteen guys in the room. Mike was the captain, and honest, I loved the kid. But when he talked to the team, it was never from the heart. It was like he sat at home and practised in the mirror. There was nothing about him or how he related to his teammates. It was like it was rehearsed and someone had given him all the lines."

In a game against Owen Sound at Maple Leaf Gardens, Futa knew it was all coming to a head. In the third period of the game, it was clear that Mike Jefferson wanted to fight the über-pest Sean Avery. "And it's funny," said Futa, "if there was one guy who could get in Avery's kitchen, it was Mike. I was looking for him on our bench and he had taken our extra chair and put it beside their bench and was giving it to Avery. They had this ongoing thing happening. They did not get along.

"But the way the game was going, I did not want Mike to fight Avery. It was clear he wanted to fight, so I kept him on the bench for a while. Then I look at the bench and Mike is gone. One of the players said, 'Frost told him to leave.' So sometime in the third period of that game, he left the bench and went to the dressing room. I think he faked an injury so he could explain to Dave why he didn't fight Avery. I'm sure he was told to fight him. But it was after that game that I knew for certain. I wasn't in control of those kids.

"We had to do something about it."

Futa met with Mark Napier and Reg Quinn, the senior executives of the St. Michael's Majors, and was asked a simple question: "Do you have control of the situation?"

"I said no.... As much it pained me, I told them, 'You've got to make a deal. We've got to trade these kids.'"

The first problem was that all four Brampton boys had no-trade arrangements in their educational contracts with St. Mike's. Futa had to go through Frost to get that cleared up. Mike Gillis may have been the agent of record for all four players, but Frost was doing all the agent's work, trying to have the players moved together in one package, seeing which teams might be interested in a deal.

"I knew we'd never get full value for the players," said Futa, "but we had determined we were making the trade and it came down to Barrie or Sudbury for the kids. We picked Barrie."

On January 11, 1999, twenty-eight games into their OHL season, the St. Michael's Majors traded Jefferson, Keefe, Cation, and Barnes to the Barrie Colts, a contending juggernaut at that time in the OHL, first coached by the legendary Bert Templeton and later by the infamous Bill Stewart. If the St. Mike's situation was an internal mess that Futa couldn't handle, the Colts became the craziest collection of players in junior hockey. For Jefferson, it was all just part of his whirlwind life in the OHL. He'd had his brief introduction to major junior hockey in Sarnia before being traded to St. Mike's, where he played the end of one season and the beginning of the next, and then was dealt to Barrie in 1999.

But long before then, OHL commissioner David Branch already knew Mike Jefferson's name from the troubling circumstances under which the rookie had left the Sarnia Sting after allegations that his relationship with Frost was somehow inappropriate. Without being introduced, though, he had shared an elevator with Dave Frost and some of the Brampton boys on the day of the OHL's Priority Selection Draft in 1997.

"We were taking the elevator down and Brian Kilrea [the Hall of Fame coach of the Ottawa 67's] was trying to get in, but the elevator was too full," said Branch. "So the doors close, and instantly this guy behind me starts badmouthing Killer [Kilrea]. He's saying stuff like that guy doesn't know anything and that guy's a joke and don't listen to that guy. And I'm thinking to myself, 'Who is this guy and who are those kids?'

"When I got off the elevator, I asked somebody, 'Do you know who that guy is?' He said yeah, that's David Frost. I stored that away and never thought about it again, until all the stories started coming out a year or so later."

The problems on the Barrie Colts were internal and external. They fought, it seemed, with everyone. One time, Sheldon Keefe was called to the OHL offices for a disciplinary hearing with Branch. Normally, a player is accompanied by a coach or another adult for such a meeting. Keefe showed up with Mike Jefferson.

"The two boys show up well—all suited up in shirts and ties— and I can remember Jefferson walking into the meeting room and he immediately attempted to take control of the situation. I was kind of taken aback, to be honest. Jefferson started to take control and I had to stop him. I said, 'Whoa. You've got this a little backwards here. You're not running this meeting. I want you to sit down and I'll ask you to speak at the right time, but now isn't the right time.'

"He was taken aback at that but he never said a word. And if looks could tell a story, he wasn't very pleased. It was interesting, though, because I'd never seen that before. I had a certain respect for what he tried to do. I was somewhat impressed that a young guy could come in here and he's going to tell us what to do. I respected it. But I didn't understand it."

From that moment on, there was a feud between Branch and the Brampton boys on the Barrie Colts, one of the many feuds that they seemed to be part of. When Barrie won the OHL championship in Plymouth in 2000, Branch called Sheldon Keefe up to get the trophy. He accepted the trophy but intentionally didn't shake the commissioner's hand.

"Obviously, I had become the bad guy with them," said Branch. "The weird thing was, Barrie had just won the championship and those boys were devoid of any emotion. That always stuck with me because I'd never seen it before."

Mike Jefferson was anything but emotionless on the ice—his name was all over the score sheet. In the playoffs, he registered nearly a point per game, along with four penalty minutes per match to round out his performance. Jefferson was impossible to miss—he was all over the ice, making things happen. But like the rest of the Colts, he was getting all kinds of attention for things other than playing hockey.

And when Barrie advanced to the Memorial Cup, the Canadian championship named in honour of fallen soldiers from World War I, their antics didn't stop. At the annual Memorial Cup banquet, held at historic Pier 21 in Halifax, where sixty thousand soldiers went off to war and never returned, the Colts couldn't help but embarrass themselves. When Branch was called up to speak, as head of the Canadian (Junior) Hockey League, there was a commotion in the room.

"The entire Barrie team got up and walked out," said Branch. "I don't know exactly what happened or why. But it was quite a statement to make. Throughout that week, I would see different players from that team and they'd come up to me and say, 'Mr. Branch, I want you to know I didn't want to do that.'

"To be honest, I put that more at the leadership of the team [coach Bill Stewart] than anyone else. But it was clear that team had all kinds of issues."

The Colts' poor behaviour was exacerbated when, prior to their tournament-opening game, a veteran in a wheelchair was brought out to drop the ceremonial faceoff and the Colts players, in defiance of ceremony, refused to line up at their blueline as is customary.

"I was ready to jump onto the ice and fight them myself," said Sherry Bassin, the junior-hockey icon, who was sixty at the time. "I don't remember ever being so mad."

That wasn't all. Barrie captain Sheldon Keefe declined to shake hands with Branch for the ceremonial opening faceoff, and during player introductions the team refused to stand at the blueline, choosing to skate around instead.

Keefe would not apologize for his slight. "If I thought it was a mistake, I wouldn't have done it," he said at the time. "It was something I felt had to be done. I don't like the way our team was treated this year. I don't respect the way our team has been handled this year by [Branch] so I acted accordingly. We got a lot of suspensions and I don't think they were warranted."

The Colts were fined $5,000 for their unruly behaviour before the first Memorial Cup game and penalized two minutes and fined again when players failed to stop skating in their zone when the "Joe Canadian" actor, then from a popular television commercial, was doing his "I Am Canadian" act. After Game 1, Jefferson made disparaging remarks about Ramzi Abid, the scoring star of the Halifax Mooseheads. In the second game, he was thrown out for fighting. Before the Colts ended up facing Rimouski in the final, Jefferson threatened their star forward, Brad Richards, claiming that the future Conn Smythe Trophy–winner wouldn't last five games in the OHL and that if he had played there, no one would have heard of him.

"When a guy like that says something like that, you have to wonder what he's talking about," said Richards. "Hopefully, he'll shut up and realize who I am." If Mike Jefferson was trying to intimidate Richards and his Rimouski teammates, it didn't work. Rimouski beat Barrie 6–2 and Richards ended up with four points in the game—two goals and two assists—and took MVP honours for the tournament. Mike Jefferson's contribution to the Colts was a major penalty and game misconduct. He refused to shake hands with Richards after the game.

And so ended what should have been a high point in Mike Jefferson's career. He'd begun major junior as a promising rookie and ended up as a point per game player on a team with a shot at claiming top honours in the country. He was on the ice at the Memorial Cup, going head to head against guys who would go on to great careers, maybe even the Hall of Fame. It was Mike Jefferson's chance to make his mark on the biggest stage of his life, a chance to put to good use all the hard work and grit that had seen him through years of early-morning practices and fuelled his dreams of hockey glory.

Instead, he let himself down. He and his team came off as boorish oafs, as graceless losers who didn't deserve to be on the ice against the class of the tournament. That would become a pattern in the years that followed—Mike coming within reach of grasping the hockey success he'd wanted so badly that he was willing to sacrifice even his parents to pursue, only to blunder badly and let it all slip away.

Strange behaviour for a guy everyone thought of as bright and disciplined—and generally decent as well. The debacle of the Memorial Cup was perhaps a sign that something ugly and self-destructive was gnawing at Mike Jefferson.

David Branch, who has seen a lot of hockey players come and go—both classy kids with great futures and thugs looking at dead ends—has his own thoughts about the issues surrounding the Colts team that was afflicted with the Brampton boys and their bizarre leader. One night, well before the Memorial Cup, Branch was walking out of Barrie's Molson Centre when he heard someone swearing at him. "It was like, 'Hey Branch, you're a fucking asshole. You're going to get it.' That kind of stuff. Very highbrow. It wasn't the first time and it won't be the last time I've heard it, but I don't take that lightly. But to be honest, thirty-two years on the job ... this was about the worst I'd heard.

"I look up as I'm getting in my truck and it was Frost. And after he yelled, he didn't face me, he proceeded into the rink. So rather than drive away, I went after him. I ran into the rink and he ran quickly in another direction. He ran away. I thought, 'Typical coward.'"

For all his years in hockey, Branch has never seen anything like the Frost–Brampton boy years in the Ontario Hockey League. He hopes to never see anything like it again.

"As a society, we continue to evolve," he said. "Some things that may have been allowed to manifest at one time won't be permitted now. If we ever see these flags again, I think it's something we'll need to address. It's unacceptable. A guy like Frost, he was trying to manufacture hockey players. He felt he had the formula to do it. And along the way, just about everybody got messed up."

July 15, 2005

Dear Mike

The year flew by for me. I'm sure it has taken forever for you.

I hope that you are not feeling like you are alone in the world because you are not. Besides, the people that you are accustomed to being your family latterly—you should know that we have a much larger crowd that is your family, that is waiting for your return.

I want to see that smile on your face again. I can show you tons of pictures of you with a big smile. Right back to being a baby. It was only when you left us that your smile went away.

I have followed your hockey and I have seen you smiling on the ice. That is what you live for.

You are young and it's not over—you have lots of support if you look in the right direction.

Love Mom

P.S.: Keep safe and write me.

[On the back of the envelope, she wrote, "Please do not forward to Dave. This is none of his business. I have supplied an envelope, paper and stamp. Write something down and send it back, okay. Please. Mom."

Also on the back of the envelope, stamped in red ink: "Inmate Refused."]

9

Draft Day and the Disappearing Dad

The NHL Entry Draft is a threshold. It's the moment careers begin and teenagers become millionaires in an instant. For teams, it represents a new beginning, a few important elements of a strategy to get to a Stanley Cup championship. It's the first day of the future.

On television, and in person, the draft is theatrical, a spectacle: the best teenaged hockey players from around the world; all dressed up in their brand new designer suits, usually purchased by their agents; all huddled nervously together with mom and dad and siblings and girlfriends and grandparents and minor-hockey coaches and old friends, with an entire sport looking on; fans and pundits all speculating on each eighteen-year-old's future, all hoping for the best for him.

It is what hockey families talk about for years. Getting drafted. Being drafted. The journey of getting there. The buildup. It has the reception line look of a wedding without any music or bride. Were this all just posing for a photograph, a stoppage of a moment in time, maybe the family portrait at the NHL draft would be something along the lines of a Norman Rockwell vision of Canada. And if not Canada, then certainly Canadian hockey.

This has been the day of reckoning for those wanting to advance in the sport. Some have described it as the most memorable day of their careers. To hear your name announced; to be called by a team; to slip on that NHL sweater for the very first time; to shake hands and pose for the photographers. It has all become a ritual. And for those fortunate enough to get there, to have their names announced, it is the first payback for all the years of family time invested in the sport, for all the money and sweat it took to build a career. Steve Jefferson rarely misses an NHL draft on television. Sometimes in his living room, usually alone, he watches and when he sees the families and the smiling faces, it all gets to him.

"I watch the kids and their families and you can see the tears in their eyes and sometimes it happens to me, too, just watching it. I sit there crying," he says. Families and their hockey players spend so much of their lives building toward the NHL Draft. But there were no televised moments, nothing captured on the big screen, not even a newspaper account of sorts, to indicate the day Mike Jefferson was drafted.

On Draft Day 2000, with the entire hockey world gathered at the Saddledome in Calgary for the grand event, with hours of national coverage planned, Steve Jefferson knew what he had to do. He disappeared for the day.

It was in fact Mike's second opportunity to be drafted. The first time, one year earlier, all thirty NHL teams passed on Mike, round after round. No one had bothered to gamble even a late-round pick on a gritty, undersized, heart-and-soul player. Mike was later invited to the Calgary Flames' rookie camp without a contract. He performed admirably in the camp and left a favourable impression on general manager Al Coates, but the Flames were tight with money and chose not to offer him a contract. That was a double rejection: no NHL squad drafted Jefferson, and the one team that would have welcomed him to its camp didn't want to sign him.

Privately, away from his son, Steve had already lived through that disappointment. He never wanted to be one of those parents—even sitting apart from his son, whatever the state of their relationship may have been—waiting and waiting for the name to be called and then not hearing it. Dreams come true on draft day, but many more are broken. For every player of promise in his youth, many more have been left behind long before draft day. But there are still a lot of players with promise who believe they have a shot, who believe enough to show up in a suit on the big day. The sad truth is that there are more such players than there are jobs in the NHL or minor-pro hockey. Every year, some of those fine young hockey players are going to go home crestfallen. The competition is too fierce. The margin is too thin between those who will have careers and those who later will talk about how close they came. Steve Jefferson didn't have the patience to wait through another five rounds of disappointment, or to relive the defeat of the previous year. There had already been enough disappointment in his life. He didn't need any more.

So on Draft Day 2000, he got into a car with his brother Jeff and drove to their cottage where there was no cable television, where he could fish and drink rather than wait around for what he figured might be more bad news. He was hoping for the best, but expecting the worst. Did Mike have a legitimate shot? True, he had been passed over again and again the year before. But he had gone back to the Colts, worked on his game, and been a big part of a team that had won the OHL title. Point-per-game players on championship teams are something scouts and GMs have to pay attention to. Steve Jefferson could see both sides of the argument. The truth was that he didn't know. And he wasn't sure he wanted to know. He turned off his mobile phone and told his good friend Brian Keefe to leave a message if anything were to happen. Sheldon Keefe had been drafted a year earlier. The two kids who had always played together were suddenly separated, one seemingly on the move and the other in limbo. This isn't the kind of draft picture you normally see on your television screen.

After a day of fishing, about five miles from the cottage, Steve Jefferson, while driving home, couldn't take it any more. He had to turn on his cellphone. His message light was flashing.

"Congratulations, brother," Brian Keefe's voice said on the message. "Mike was drafted by the New Jersey Devils in the fifth round."

Being drafted in the fifth round assures nothing for the player but an opportunity to make the big time. A fifth-round pick has a shot at a career, but only a shot. It's a life-support system for dreams. If you're like Mike Jefferson, the 135th player taken in what's considered a fairly average draft class, you've got nothing more than a 10 percent chance of making the big time and staying there. On average, three out of the thirty players chosen in the fifth round of an entry draft have careers of any length. The rest? The rest are forgotten.

Mike Jefferson was always considered something of a long shot, almost from the time he started playing. His size worked against him, as he played a big man's game in a smaller man's body. To understand the difficulty involved in even making an NHL lineup, consider this: When Jefferson and Keefe played for the very successful Barrie Colts, five of their teammates were first-round picks of NHL teams. Only one of them, defenceman Martin Skoula, made a lasting jump to the NHL. If the players the thirty NHL teams kept at the top of their lists had such a hard time making it, what were the chances for a guy they had all passed over several times?

But that's not where Steve Jefferson's mind was at. He was thinking about the cold morning drives to the rink, the tournaments, the evenings on the couch watching *Hockey Night in Canada*. That one phone message, and the news it conveyed, distilled years of willing sacrifice and hard-fought dreams.

"And as soon as he said it, I broke down crying. I don't know if I heard the rest of the message. If I did, I don't remember what else he said," Steve remarked. "My brother looked at me and he said, 'He got drafted, eh.' And all I could say was, 'New Jersey, fifth round.' And I couldn't stop bawling. My heart was racing. I'm crying and I'm yelling in the car, 'Mike's going to the fucking New Jersey Devils.' And I just kept yelling and yelling. I knew this was Mike's last real shot. I was so happy for him, so excited for him."

Steve's first phone call was to his best friend and fellow hockey dad, Keefe. They had lived through so much together, shared so many hockey experiences. "I was ecstatic. I was just so excited."

His second phone call was to his wife. "He was crying, trying to get the words out," said Sue. "He was all choked up. It was a short conversation." Sue hung up the phone. She was proud and excited for her son, and just a little sad for herself. She had always been the hockey outsider—here was the greatest moment of her son's career and she was at home, away from the draft, away from her son, away from her husband. Alone.

"I was kind of left out of the whole hockey thing," said Sue. "The girls [mothers of players] were always told, 'Mind your own business.' That's pretty much how it was. We were kind of isolated from it. I think a lot of the mothers felt that way.

"On draft day, I was excited and proud. It would have been nice to have been there and been part of it. But you have to realize, even if we were there, we wouldn't have been there, if you know what I mean. There wouldn't have been any acknowledgment. We would have been outsiders. That might have felt worse than not being part of it at all."

Steve Jefferson hardly remembers the car ride home from the cottage. It's all a blur of sorts now ... of greetings and phone calls and messages and emotions and confusion and the occasional drink. "I couldn't go, didn't want to go to the draft. I was too superstitious to go. I didn't want the possible letdown. The year before hadn't worked out and Dave Frost seemed to think Michael was going to get drafted this time. He didn't know when or which team, but he figured this was going to be his year. And when he was drafted, Frost came back into the house, his chest out, kind of doing the 'I told you so' thing."

On Draft Day 2000, everything changed—everything but the father–son thing. The one call Steve didn't make was to his son. And the one he didn't receive was from Mike. On the day they had dreamed of, the day they had sacrificed everything for, the two men could find nothing to say to each other. Mike was with Frost. Steve fished and drank and eventually made his way home. This was no Rockwell painting.

A few days later, Mike Jefferson came home, but not for long.

"When Mike came in, I congratulated him, hugged him, told him how proud I was of him," says Steve, fighting to keep his emotions in check. "It was a proud moment for me.

"A few minutes later, he walked out the door and walked back to Dave's house."

Steve and Mike Jefferson had spent years scrapping to get to the NHL. They may not have talked much. And by the time Mike had a big-league contract, they may not have had much to do with each other at all—Mike had Mike Gillis and Dave Frost to take care of things. But the Jeffersons still shared something. Whether they talked to each other or not, father and son still shared the dream they talked about during their drives to the rink.

Steve certainly never forgot that. At the end of Mike's first pro training camp, a camp in which he performed beyond expectations and clearly made a statement that he could one day be an NHL player, he was sent to the Albany River Rats, the Devils' American Hockey League farm team. That isn't uncommon for a young player, especially a rookie who's a fifth-round pick. Young players don't usually show up in the NHL ready to play in the season opener. They almost always need minor-pro ice time, and that's what Mike was sent to Albany to get. But he had certainly left an impression: he was going to factor in the Devils' future.

The first game Mike ever played for Albany, Steve Jefferson and his brother Jeff drove all the way from Toronto to see him play. He didn't tell Mike he was coming to the game, nor did he wait afterwards for him. He knew he had to be there and not be noticed. "I didn't want to be a distraction," said Steve. "I just had to be there for his first pro game. After all we'd been through, I had to be there." That was in the fall of 2000, just a few months after Mike had been selected in the entry draft.

But if Steve clung to hopes that the realization of their shared dream might resuscitate his relationship with his son, he was doomed to still more disappointment. Instead of making things better, Mike's fledgling success only made them worse. When Mike signed a contract worth more than $1 million with the Devils, and $75,000 just as a signing bonus, the money caused trouble right away. Soon, Steve began hearing rumours that he had been clamouring for his share of Mike's money.

"Somehow, Dave got it into Michael's head that I wanted a piece of the bonus. And that seemed to end our relationship. I don't know what Mike signed for. I was never party to it. I don't know what he got. I know what I got. Nothing. And I never asked for anything, any money, nothing.

"One of the times Dave was being investigated, a cop told me that he'd heard I asked Mike for money to pay my income tax. Supposedly, I told Michael I needed $50,000 to pay the tax. The cop told me that was the story going around. That didn't happen. I never asked Mike for any money at all. That's just bullshit. But Dave had apparently told him that and whatever Dave told him, he believed. And after that, if I ever tried to talk to Mike, Dave would intercept. He'd tell me not to bother him any more. That Mike's concentrating on hockey. That he didn't want to talk to me."

Steve Jefferson spent the first year of his son's pro career this way—reaching out and being rebuffed. By the beginning of the 2001–02 season, Mike's second year as a pro, nothing had changed between father and son. The father still called; the son still turned away. But that year, something happened in New York that demanded a phone call. When the Twin Towers were attacked, Steve Jefferson became preoccupied with his son's welfare at the Devils' training camp. He worried, like everyone worried, about the safety of living in the New York area.

A few days after 9/11, he phoned his son because he felt he had to. The Devils were on a bus heading to New York to play the Rangers in an exhibition game. He wanted to hear Mike's voice. The cellphone rang on the Devils' bus and Mike answered. "Dad,

I can't talk," he said. "We're going across the bridge to play the Rangers. I'll talk to you later."

The next day, Steve Jefferson picked up the morning paper and smiled when he saw a photograph of his son playing opposite Eric Lindros. He held the picture. His wife clipped it for their scrapbook.

The last words they ever spoke came from the cellphone on the team bus. "I'll talk to you later," said Mike Jefferson.

They never did.

December 7, 2005

Dear Mike

Please forgive me for not writing as often as I would like. It's been hard to receive the letters back. It breaks my heart.

I want you to know that we are still fighting very hard against that monster—Dave. We will win.

I will not let him get you again. You will never have to worry about his control anymore. The whole world, literally, is tuned into this. You have more support than you can even imagine.

Do not listen to a word that monster Dave says. There isn't anything that comes out of his mouth that's meant for the better of you.

Just be strong and patient—it's almost over.

The important thing now is to get on the road to recovery and get you back on track. Please contact me somehow. I miss you. I can't wait to see you.

Love Mom

[The letter was torn into little pieces; the envelope was stamped "Return to sender" and the address was crossed out.]

10

The Christmas Treatise

In December of 2000, with Mike Jefferson living in Albany and playing in the American Hockey League, Sheldon Keefe living in Tampa and playing in the NHL, and the rest of the Brampton boys scattered throughout the various levels of pro and university hockey, Dave Frost sat down and wrote a letter to his troops.

Really, it was more than just a letter. It was something of a manual, a treatise of sorts, on how to live your life and how he viewed their relationships.

He sent it out to the boys in his inner circle and printed on the cover was a note saying that a copy was being sent to Mike Gillis, too.

The words here are Frost's. So are the spelling, punctuation, and grammatical errors. The typewritten letter has not been edited in any way from the original one that he sent out, a copy of which was found by Sue Jefferson while she was cleaning in her home.

Xmas 2000, this is some thing I'v wanted to do for a long time, and finally here it is.. .

Please read this from time to time when your in need of advice or at least once a year, this is from me to you and this, in my opinion, is the most important gift I could ever givc any of you, share this with your future children or wife if you like or keep it for your sell'as personal guide to better living and the real world, I have gathered thoughts that I think are important to say or will be soon in all of yqur lives. We are all going to start to do are ownseparate things and its important to rerperitber that we will nevr ever separate but we will ileed to be able to stand on our own to feet, REMEMBERING that we will never stand alone, we have a bond that can not be broken ever.. . . . .

Character

I believe that it is this.to which your life is deterniined and live with the knowledge that your character is your destiny.

friendship

I believe that this is the most important thing we all have, most people search all there lives for the type of friends we have in each other, never and I mean ever do you forget about the friends you have , no matter what the situation, nothing, not money , not a hot blonde, nothing can replace your friends ever, when you wake up one day and realize this (and you will) you will see that this can never be replaced ever, and we all have some thing that will keep us together 4 ever and its that bond of friendship that we all were apart of building, all of us. we did it , we built it, we must keep it, vic would never let a little dispute injure our friendship right?, so lets think about building this into our lives everyday, I propose that every xmas starting next year we all come together, no matter what, one place one time, doesn't matter where we are, but one of us can not be there, all of us must be there.

Who you marry

Its funny I always thought that I would be in on this , but i

n reality , it's only you who can tell the rest of us , if this

personis the one !!, BUT, live by these rules and you will be

always happy. . . . . . .

Marry some one who has values, that wants you for who you are and does not iry to change you at all, unless you want to, and only you. Remember if that person trys to make you choose between them and your friends, then that person is not the one , she onlv J cares about herself and it will never work ever no matter how hard you try, remember there are a lot of girls out there, never think, that you can't find another, trust me you always kill, and you have to remember that this person will raise your .A. --? child and you will grow oia together, so you must be able to talk to them your conversations will be key to happiness.Live and be engaged for atleast a year, then you will hiow, never ever hit or even consider violence in a fight , use your mind, fight fair don't bring up the past , or her family back ground, only be smart, and think before you talk, when you say I love you mean it! !, don't believe in love at first sight, some times silence is the best answer, make sure your home is loving when you have kids they will sense it, your kids have to be the most important thing C/ in your life when you have them, if there not, don't have them, they must be always number 1 to you, take the job o E there up bringing to heart, there are enough bad fucks in this world, make yours smart , loving , with character, aware of the world, remember some one helped you! !, help them pass it on... Its funny , I have installed as much as I can in all of you and still feel at times I have failed. But its you that has some thing inside of you that makes you who you are , your good people and you r' care follow that and remember that this world is not fair, you must be strong arid be ready to take it on , disipline yourself to be strong tough and kill before your killed, this world is there for you to take, you must take it

On this next page I have written some quick things for you to read, really read it! ! ! ! ! ! ! ! ! !

1. judge your success by what you had to give up in order to b set it

2.if you make a lot of moneyput it to use helping others while you are living, if they deserve it, wealths great when its shared

3.mind your own business

4. Learn the rules so you know how to break them properly

5.share your knoledge

6. Read more books than tv

7. Spend some time alone

8. Open your arms to change, but don't let go of your values

9.follow the three R'S.. respect yourself', respect those who deserve it, responsibility for all your actions i \

10. If you don't have dreams you have nothing ?

11. When some one asks you a question you - . % , . L don't want to answer, smiie and ask" why do want to know"

12. When you say your sorry look the person in the eye

13 .don't believe all you hear, choose your self

14.teach yourself to speak slowly.. but to think quickly

15.remember to be on guard on the road or out and about

16.trust those who deserve to be trusted

17. Respect is never given

18. Nothing is free you must earn everything

19.always remember those who help you, and if you can return the favour one day do it !!

20. when I'm gone remember everything , not just the good thing-sltimes, remember everything, that's where your knowledge came from, I hope this finds you each time you read it safe and happy, and always look on the smart side of things. Take care of all the people in your life that mean some thing to you, not who others think, mom, dad, whoever, i& who you think that matters and counts remember return the favour and protect your children.

11

The Agent Who Couldn't Let Go

David Frost promised Mike Jefferson that he would make the National Hockey League one day. All Mike had to do was listen to him. Listen to everything. Follow him. Do what he was told.

And it worked. Jefferson was drafted by the Stanley Cup champion New Jersey Devils in 2000. He seemed headed in the right direction as a hockey player.

Frost orchestrated things. He kept his promise by pushing and pulling, working levers, pulling strings. It was as though Mike Jefferson was his marionette, doing exactly what Frost wanted him to do and going where they both wanted him to go. But the puppet master could never let go of the strings.

"Frost always said, 'My job is to get them to the NHL and then I'll let them go,'" said Mike Futa.

"When you met with Dave, he would always make the comment, 'I just want to take these guys and drop them off at the dance. They're going to be pros and it's my goal to get them there.' But he couldn't drop them off at the dance. He wanted to attend the dance. And he wanted to talk to all the new chaperones. And he wanted to be involved with everything that was going on.

"Give Dave credit. He said he was going to get those kids to the NHL, and he got Sheldon and Mike there—and Barnes came close, played a couple of games in Detroit. He said he'd do it and he did it. And if you consider the odds, that's pretty remarkable. But he couldn't let go. That ended up damaging him and damaging them. That's the part that's a shame. His whole speech, whether you believed it or not, I just want to get them there and let these guys alone, never happened. He couldn't back away. He couldn't stop controlling things.

"It was a little different with Sheldon. He had immense talent. I think Sheldon would have played [in the NHL] no matter who coached him. It was different with Mike. Mike was his guy. Mike had to work for everything he got. He had to outwork people. He had to out-train people. He had great intensity and a high level of competitiveness. You can say Frost got him there, by whatever means, and you don't have to like his ways, but he got him to the NHL.

"And really, I think once he did, he started playing a part in ruining their careers."

A year before the Devils drafted Mike Jefferson, they had already taken a keen interest in the budding player. In fact, they invited Jefferson to come to New Jersey to meet with their scouting staff, go through a series of physical tests and interviews—the kinds of things draft prospects submit to every year. But for whatever reason, Jefferson, through his agent Mike Gillis, declined the invitation. "We didn't understand it, but that was their prerogative," said David Conte, the Devils' assistant general manager and director of scouting. "We had some questions about [Frost] and some other things. But when Mike didn't show up, we moved on."

One year later, after being passed over in the 1999 NHL entry draft, Conte again invited Jefferson to what the Devils called a "satellite camp" in Minnesota. This time, he showed up.

"We had some questions for him," said Conte, who is Lou Lamoriello's right-hand man in New Jersey. "We didn't know an awful lot about David Frost, but we had heard about him. We had to ask. Mike had those problems at the Memorial Cup and we wanted to talk about that.

"But from the time we first met, I think he was almost the opposite of what we expected. I really liked the kid. To this day, I can honestly say I like him. He's very likeable. I think if he was less suspicious of others, of almost everything, everybody would like him. But because of who he was, I wanted to spend time to get to know him. I have to be honest—I was absolutely captivated by how engaging, intelligent, considerate he was. We went out to dinner two or three times. He seemed like a wonderful young man to me, and I still think deep down, that's in him.

"I didn't see anything that you would even consider to be a major cause for concern. He talked a lot about the home he grew up in. He spoke openly about his father's demons with alcohol. I've interviewed a lot of hockey players over the years. I can tell you a lot of kids who made it grew up in worse homes than he did."

Conte was so impressed with Jefferson that when the Devils put their list together for the 2000 draft in Calgary, they had him rated as a late second-round pick. Conte, thrilled with the selection, wound up choosing him in the fifth round. The Devils had a boatload of picks that year and wanted to cash in big with them. They wound up taking defenceman David Hale in the first round; four players, including blueliner Paul Martin, in the second round; Michael Rupp in the third round (he went on to score a Stanley

Cup–winning goal); and with their ninth selection, Jefferson. Even though Jefferson's career was cut short because of jail time, he still managed to play more NHL games than four of the Devils' choices before him as well as nine of the thirty players selected in the 2000 draft's first round by other NHL teams—those players expected to be pretty close to sure things.

"We thought we got a steal. I believe we did," said Conte. "Scouting is a lot like baseball. If you're batting .300, you're doing pretty well. If you get a good player in the fifth round, that's a bonus. To us, Mike Jefferson was a bonus."

And when camp opened, Mike continued to turn heads.

"Mike had come in, worked hard, never shortchanged himself," said Devils boss Lou Lamoriello. "His work ethic was extreme. He minded his own business. You wouldn't know he was here, he was so quiet, except he made some noise on the ice. At the beginning, there were no issues with him whatsoever."

At the beginning.

The honeymoon ended when Jefferson was told he was being sent to the Albany River Rats—the Devils' minor-league affiliate. He may have been a rookie, a fifth-round pick trying to crack the lineup of the Stanley Cup champions. But rejection wasn't something he was prepared for.

"What surfaced immediately were little things. He thought there were reasons he didn't make it," said Lamoriello. "I tried to explain that all players need to grow and the best place to grow is in the minor leagues.

"With Mike, it was never anything we couldn't tolerate. And [the late] John Cunniff, Albany's head coach, said he could handle it. But there were problems throughout the year with him. There were always questions. He was asking about ice time, and that's

BROTHERS

Brothers: Sheldon Keefe (left), Mike Jefferson (centre), and Ryan Barnes (right) in their Barrie Colts days. All three would be drafted by NHL teams that went on to win the Stanley Cup, though none ended up with a ring.

In happier times:
Mike posing on an
amusement park ride
for a portrait.

What a horrible childhood:
Mike smiling with Santa.

Mike playing for the Young Nats, one of the most storied hockey programs in the country.

The Quinte Six: Mike Jefferson is in the middle, with David Frost right behind him. The team's behaviour on and off the ice attracted the attention of the police more than once.

Ontario Champs: The
Young Nats win it all.
(David Frost is circled.)

Mike Jefferson, proud
member of the Toronto
Red Wings. He may not
have got the ice time he
wanted, but his play drew
the attention of David
Frost.

Real brothers: Mike and Tom as young kids. Hockey brought the family together, then tore it apart.

The Brampton boys in their St. Mike's jackets: from left, Shawn Cation, Sheldon Keefe, and Mike Jefferson.

Grade 8 at Williams Parkway School. Mike is at the far left of the middle row. Mike was always known as a bright, tractable student.

Head on a swivel: Even in Mike's rookie season of minor hockey, his father knew he had the will to go far.

In better times: Mike and Tom beaming as they sit with a young cousin.

Mike, Tom, and Grandpa. As usual, Mike is wearing something hockey-related.

The family Mike said he didn't have. That's Mike in the middle with the big smile.

Tom Jefferson begged his parents to go, but a week at David Frost's cottage would haunt him for years. (Courtesy Joe Warmington)

David Frost as he appeared in his high-school yearbook.

Tom Jefferson playing for the Oshawa Generals. He had the talent to go as far as his brother did.

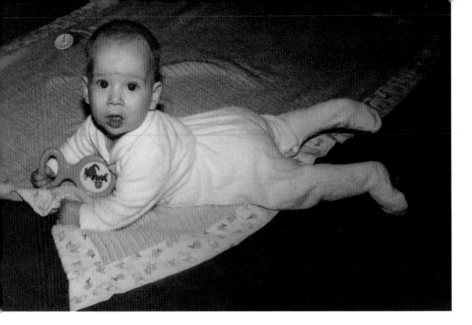

Baby Mike.

Mike and Steve Jefferson in their chair, watching hockey.

The Keefes and Jeffersons do Florida. That's Tom Jefferson and Adam Keefe in the white T-shirts.

Mike heading to an out-of-town tournament.

Young Mike Jefferson with the Chinguacousy Blues. Mike quickly moved to the GTHL looking for stiffer competition.

Mike with the Barrie Colts. A series of trades landed him on a serious contender for the Memorial Cup, but the tempestuous Colts fared poorly in the spotlight.

A handsome young Mike Jefferson.

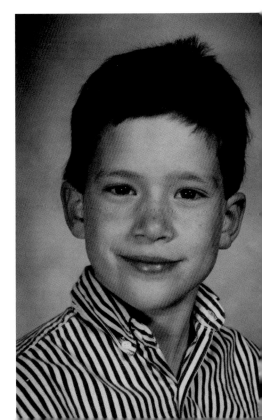

Mike Jefferson's tournament ID from the 1996 Kobe Cup.

Happy Birthday: Tom with Mike, Steve, and Sue at the kitchen table. It would not be long before it was all but unimaginable for all four to be at the same table.

Mike and Dad
heading out on
the road.

More young Mike.

Mike Danton in his last NHL season, playing for the St. Louis Blues. He had dreamed his whole life of playing in the world's top league, but didn't stay there long.

something you don't hear about from a young player very often. He was asking about what line he was on, or how he was being used—just things most hockey players don't ask about, especially as rookies. It was like someone was telling him to ask those questions because I don't believe he would have asked them on his own.

"You have to understand something. John Cunniff was a very mature, very experienced coach. And we talked on almost a daily basis. There was always something about Jefferson that would come up. John felt there were some irregularities in some of his behaviours. What everybody noticed was that he was always on the phone. The minute the game ended, he was on the phone. The minute the practice ended, he was on the phone. He was never late for the bus or anything. I don't know who he was talking to on the phone, but over time I've assumed it had to be Frost. It was different. We knew the way he was a loner, the way he didn't mix with the other guys, the way he was always whispering in his phone. It made people uncomfortable."

Also different was the relationship Mike had established with Conte. It was clear that Jefferson, who trusted hardly anyone, trusted Conte. If he had a problem, a question, something he needed settled, he would call Conte.

And he would call often.

"There was always this feeling that whatever he was getting, it wasn't enough," said Conte. The questions kept coming. Conte often wondered where they came from. "He would call me and say, 'I should be getting called up' or 'I should be playing more' or 'Why am I not playing with this guy?' or 'Why am I used in that role?' It's not uncommon for players to feel that way. Most at that stage don't act on their feelings, or someone [an agent] asks for them.

"I always told him, 'If you ask me a question, I will go to Lou and get the answer. You may not like the answer but if you want it, I will get you an answer.'"

What Lamoriello didn't know at the time, and found out later, was that Frost was living in Albany with his wife and kids in Jefferson's home. "That was not typical," said Lamoriello. "In fact, in all my time in hockey, I've never heard of an arrangement like that. I didn't really find out about it until the end of the season."

"I never heard a word from David Frost," said Conte, "but you knew he was there. I thought the questions were coming from him. And it was clear to us that as well as he was contributing on the ice, Mike wasn't fitting in within the confines of the family structure that is apparent with the Devils. He was a marginal role player with things to prove, but sometimes he acted like he was entitled."

If there is one thing that rubs hockey people the wrong way, it's a sense of entitlement. John Cunniff was a career hockey man who had coached and played at almost every level. But he'd never come across anything quite like Jefferson before.

Still, Cunniff decided to give Mike Jefferson some rope. He saw the talent in him, and tried to make him part of the Devils' family. More than most professional hockey teams, the Devils have their own way, their own identity. They have a style of play, a style of decorum, an expectation many teams don't foist on their players. The Devils have been the private school of NHL teams. More rules, more uniforms, more discipline than most. But it didn't work for Jefferson. "When we had our post-season meeting with John, and we went over all the players, a lot of things surfaced. Things we tried to address in the summer. We wanted Mike to change," said Lamoriello.

"We wanted him to be with us, not against us. Sometimes he did things, like he was acting on someone else's instructions. You'd be in a game, and you'd be winning, and for some reason he felt it necessary to fight, almost like someone else was telling him to fight. He would do things like that. He wasn't a teammate, he was an individual. We tried to make him part of our family."

Jefferson, already estranged from his birth family, wasn't quite ready to be part of the Devils' family either.

If the first year in Albany was troubling for Lamoriello, the second season was almost unexplainable. Again, Jefferson had a decent training camp, impressed the coaching staff and thought he should have been part of coach Pat Burns's team. But on the last day of training camp, Lamoriello sat down with Jefferson to tell him he was again being sent back to Albany. Jefferson did not take the news well.

When Lamoriello called him in to go over the details, the conversation took a turn he didn't expect. A day or two earlier, he had spoken with Jefferson's agent, Mike Gillis. Everything seemed to be all right. Gillis expected the demotion. There are very few sure bets on the fourth line of an NHL team.

"I'll never forget that day," said Lamoriello. "I told him what was going down and I said, 'Listen, I'll talk to your representative [Gillis]. He'll take care of things.'

"Mike said, 'He's not my representative any more.'

"This kind of surprised me. I had just spoken to Gillis a day or two earlier. 'When did this happen?' I asked him.

"'I'm firing him now,'" said Jefferson.

"I called Mike Gillis back. The firing was news to me; it was news to him...."

Mike Jefferson's new agent of record: Dave Frost.

Upset at being demoted to the minors when he fully expected to play for the Devils, Jefferson was suspended for refusing to report to Albany. "He just left," said Lamoriello. "He said he was going to California because he wanted to be a movie actor or something like that. David Frost had taken over as his agent and to this point, I still hadn't met him or spoken to him. I didn't think of this at the time, but Mike Gillis and I have talked about this since. When he fired Gillis, he was actually doing Gillis a favour."

David Conte believes that if Jefferson was left on his own, he would have made very different hockey decisions. But Conte found him incapable of taking control of his own life. Jefferson could only blame others for his problems.

"The idea that he was taking his ball and going home just wasn't acceptable. And it went against almost everything he did when playing," said Conte. "He wasn't a quitter; he was a fearless player with a tremendous work ethic. He was an amazing physical specimen. I never thought there was any quit in Mike, but he never took control of his life. He would find fault with others. There was this little bit of immaturity about him, or certainly self-centredness. That was bothersome. He looked at it like he was the only player on the team sometimes. It was odd for a role player to have that kind of attitude."

Mike Jefferson's behaviour was becoming increasingly erratic. He was thumbing his nose at arguably the top team in the league, turning his back on hockey, and wandering off to California. This was not the behaviour of a kid hell-bent on making it in the NHL. But one thing from that year stands out as a defining moment in the story of this troubled young player. For reasons that have never completely been explained, Mike Jefferson changed his name to Mike Danton. If there was separation between him and his family before, the name change made it official. Mike wanted a new name, a new identification, a fresh start, a divorce from his biological parents. In a way, there was a line drawn in the sand: Frost on one side; his family on the other side. He needed to make a declaration on his future. Instead of taking the name of Frost, he chose the name of Danton, which belonged to a kid he remembered from hockey-school days. He changed his middle name also, losing the Stephen part of his name and adding Sage, further distancing himself from his father.

Mike Jefferson didn't play a professional hockey game in the 2001–02 season, but the Devils, owning his professional rights, were not willing to give up on him. Not yet, anyhow.

The Devils were an excellent team in 2002–03, the best in the NHL. And after a year away from the game, Mike Danton, with a new name, and maybe a new attitude, and having lost his grievance, had made the team out of training camp. He was finally where he wanted to be, trying to fit in, listening to his coaches. It was as if the new name and the year off—by this time the Devils didn't know what to expect next from him—had given him a fresh start. Lou Lamoriello noticed a difference from the beginning of that camp: He saw a better player, a more desperate player, maybe a player who decided in his year away from hockey that this was all he had. Even with a year away from the game, Danton came to training camp in marvellous condition. If determination was always his calling card, suddenly he had turned it up a notch.

When the season began, his career was finally going in the right direction. Without the legendarily annoying Bobby Holik in the lineup, the Devils needed an agitator, and Mike Danton fit the bill. He was doing what he did best: skating hard, hitting, agitating, drawing penalties. He even managed to spice up an already heated rivalry with the New York Rangers by knocking Pavel Bure out of the lineup with a hit that outraged the Rangers and provoked Mark

Messier to challenge him to a fight. The next time the two teams met, the normally unflappable Rangers goalie Mike Richter took a two-handed swing at Danton with his stick.

"I guess he didn't like that I was standing in front of his net," said Danton disingenuously after the game.

"He does what he has to do to make the team, but there's more to hockey than yapping," Richter complained to the media. But Danton and the New Jersey Devils must have been thinking that if the Rangers' superstar goalie—winner of both a Stanley Cup and a World Cup—was thinking and complaining about Mike Danton, the kid from Brampton was doing his job just fine.

And Danton could do more than annoy world-class goalies. In his second game of the season, his fourth career game in the big time, he scored the first goal of his NHL career on October 12, 2002: the Devils' home opener. The goal came at 13:49 of the first period against Marc Denis of the Columbus Blue Jackets to tie the game 1–1. The Devils went on to win 3–2 at the Meadowlands.

"On the one hand, we were concerned about him. And on the other hand we were impressed by what he could do for us," said Lamoriello. "This is what we do for our players. We want them to be able to fit in as best they can. We were willing to fight for Mike."

When the season began, Lamoriello had a plan for the young man now named Danton. He decided to room him on the road with different veteran Devils players, people he thought would be a good influence on him. This is what teams do when they are concerned about certain players. "To be honest, it was very difficult for anyone to reach him," said Lamoriello. "No matter who his roommate was, there was always someone more influential at any given time. Mike was always respectful, never challenging to the point of doing anything foolish, but there was always something missing.

"He couldn't wait to get out of the locker room after practice or games. He was always on the phone. The players didn't know what to make of him. They couldn't understand what he was doing, who he was talking to. After a while, it became something people talked about, a distraction of sorts. As hard as he worked as a player, it was like there was this phone attached to him. Nothing could get in the way of the phone call."

Eventually, the Devils had to act. After seventeen games with the team, and too many phone calls to remember, Lamoriello summoned Danton to his office and told him he was being sent back to Albany. For Danton, that was the hockey equivalent of a death sentence. He would not, could not, accept it and refused the assignment.

"We suspended him when he didn't report to the minors," said Lamoriello. "First, he didn't report. Then he claimed he was injured and filed a grievance with the players' union."

It was during that time Danton spoke these now-famous words: "I'm not going to drink Lou's Kool-Aid"—a reference to the apparent cult of the Devils and the infamous tragedy of the Jonestown suicides in Guyana.

Danton told the *Newark Star Ledger*, "I worked my butt off for this team. I haven't done anything wrong.... Obviously, I don't fit in here. Maybe I have to cut my hair a different length or shave more." He never did return to the Devils.

During the suspension, Lamoriello got to know Dave Frost on the telephone, as much as anyone ever gets to know him.

"He would call often," said Lamoriello. "The calls were always calm at the beginning but they didn't last that way. He would become very abusive and threatening. But that never affected me. I never responded to him that way. I never allow emotion to get involved in a decision. I had no reason to be combative. I felt we were dealing with a young player who had potential. He could have been an asset to our organization. Maybe, he was a little bit disturbed. But I think the advice he was getting wasn't helping him. Whatever control it was that Frost had over him didn't seem to be helping Mike any. I fought hard to get Mike back. We had nothing against him personally. The way I approach it, our team is more important than any one individual."

The back and forth between Frost and Lamoriello says much about Frost's unwillingness or inability to respect authority figures. Frost, to use his words, didn't "give a shit" who he was dealing with. He was going to play the bully role no matter what, even if he met his match in the legendary Lamoriello, one of the wisest, most respected, and probably most steadfast leaders in all of hockey. But Frost could never see beyond his own unstable ambition. And sometimes Danton would fall into a similar trap.

On more than one occasion, Danton called Lamoriello himself from California to talk about coming back. During some of the calls, Lamoriello got the impression that Danton wasn't on the phone alone. "One time, I had a conversation with him and he thought I hung up. And I hear him say to someone, 'I think he just hung up on me.' And I heard another voice. It was confirming something I had thought previously on other calls. I had the strong feeling that David Frost was listening in on our conversation. Honestly, I believe that to be true."

To this day, the New Jersey Devils management feels as though it failed Mike Danton almost as much as the player failed himself.

"When I look back, I think, 'Look how close Mike was to playing for us.' Like a lot of players, we wanted him to learn how to play at the minor-league level," says Lamoriello. "We do that with lots of our players. I always say it's better to bring someone up too late rather than too soon. With Mike, it was never personal. It was just difficult. You'd talk to him and you know the player isn't talking to you. Someone else is.

"If he had played the way his abilities allowed him to, I think he would have had a long and very successful career. That kind of irritating player is a help to any team. And if it didn't happen with us, it should have happened, would have happened, with another NHL team."

The Devils team that Mike Danton walked out on, to supposedly become an actor, wound up winning the Stanley Cup in 2003. The kid from Brampton should have been a Stanley Cup winner. "Who knows," says Lamoriello. "That's something we'll never know."

But Danton had gone out of his way to cut all ties with the team. In fact, he went so far as to send the Devils the puck with which he had scored his first NHL goal, claiming he didn't need it any more. "I've got my first puck at home on the shelf and I'm very proud of it," says former teammate Sergei Brylin. "I don't know what he's thinking about."

Twelve days after winning the Stanley Cup, and almost three years to the day after Danton was drafted by the Devils, Lamoriello traded Mike Danton to the St. Louis Blues on June 21, 2003. New Jersey got a third-round pick in return. The trade barely garnered a headline.

But the Devils GM never forgot the kid he had tried to groom into a bona fide NHLer.

"I was truly saddened," said Lamoriello years later of the news that the player he'd plucked in the draft had been arrested for a felony. "And I was shocked. I felt extremely bad for Mike. I don't know what happened to get him in that state. You never know what's going through someone's mind. You don't know what pressures they are under or what problems they are facing. You read or hear about that, you take a step back and say, 'You think you get to know someone as a person but you really don't.' There were a lot of good qualities about Mike but there was also something that always seemed wrong about him—something that always put him in a different way, a different light.

"I don't know if any of us can understand what happened with him and Frost. But unless you've experienced it, even from our end, it's very hard to explain. It's not exaggerated. It was there, very noticeable to our people and our players. The word I would use is *bizarre*. All my life in hockey, I'd never seen anything like it. The whole experience was just not normal."

Danton's jail term, which ostensibly ended his NHL career, also saddened David Conte, once his greatest advocate within the Devils family and the pro hockey executive closest to him from before he was drafted to the moment he was traded to St. Louis.

"The story is a tragic one you wouldn't wish on anyone," said Conte. "The hard part for me is that in many ways I very much respected Mike. I liked him. His life was like a script you wouldn't believe and I don't know anyone who would have had the imagination to think this up. To this day, I just feel like this was a waste of talent. Did he have a fair chance in life? I don't know.

"Personally, I feel like I failed him to some degree. He was heading down a self-destructive path and we knew it. And we tried to do something about it. I don't know if I failed him personally or we failed him collectively. But it seems to me that everyone who has played a role in his life has failed him. And most importantly, he failed himself.

"In the end, I think it was the OHL's fault, the NHL's fault, the police's fault, the New Jersey Devils' fault, the NHLPA's fault, Bob Goodenow's fault, his parents' fault. Ultimately, the price was paid by Mike Danton. A lot of people failed this kid and he failed himself."

Sheldon Keefe was supposed to be a first-round pick in the 1999 NHL entry draft. Just about everybody thought so. He was one of those natural talents, skilled offensively with a good head for the game, and a real competitive side to him. Years earlier, Bob Goodenow had nicknamed him The Professor, because he took everything in and had an intelligence that many hockey players seem to lack. The only caveat to his blossoming career: he was one of Dave Frost's kids.

At the 1999 draft, Tampa Bay general manager Rick Dudley felt strongly about Keefe's talents. If he could get him, Dudley wanted him. And as the draft began to take shape and the first picks were made, it was apparent there was a certain unease about taking Keefe too high, a gamble teams were unwilling to take. General managers wanted Keefe, but something was holding them back.

"I do recall there being quite a bit of discussion at our draft table about Sheldon," says Jay Feaster, who was assistant general manager of the Lightning at the time. "Sheldon kept dropping and dropping. We saw a lot of players picked who weren't better than him. There was a lot of discussion and a lot of concern. We knew the reason he was dropping. Everybody knew. And finally Rick Dudley said, 'This is ridiculous. We're taking this kid.'"

The Lightning selected Sheldon Keefe with the forty-seventh pick.

That was Jay Feaster's introduction to the most talented of the Brampton boys. His introduction to Dave Frost would come shortly thereafter.

"I remember meeting with Mike Gillis, Sheldon's agent. We met a couple of times in my office. Right in the middle of our conversation, his phone would ring and he'd take a look at it and shake his head. He wouldn't pick up. Then a few minutes later, it would ring again. When it happened a few more times, Mike later told me it was Frost calling. Frost had to know what was going on.

"Then later, over the next few years, some strange things would happen. The Lightning would get a call from some small-town newspaper in Ontario, with the guy on the phone claiming to be a reporter. When we'd give the information to our PR department, they would find out that the guy didn't exist or the newspaper didn't exist, but each time we got one of those calls the subject was always Sheldon Keefe. 'What are your plans for Sheldon?' 'Don't you think Sheldon should be playing?' It's about the strangest thing I've seen in all my years in hockey.

"Then, when I became GM [in 2002], I would get calls directly from Frost. He was what I would call a constant presence. The questions were always the same: 'Why isn't Sheldon playing with Vinny [Lecavalier]?' 'Why isn't Sheldon a top-six forward?' 'Why isn't Sheldon getting more ice time?' 'Why isn't coach [John] Tortorella using him more?'

"The thing about Sheldon is, he's a good kid. He was a talented player and a tenacious player, the kind of player who wasn't afraid to go into traffic and score goals. He was a fearless player. But he was just at the beginning of his professional-development stage."

And like Mike Danton, he was impatient—or Frost was impatient. One thing Feaster is absolutely certain about, Frost was doing Keefe no favours by haranguing Lightning management. The more he questioned the temperamental John Tortorella, the less willing the coach was to give Keefe any kind of opportunity. Feaster also worried about Keefe's ability to fit in with the team.

"I remember a particular day during training camp in Florida, we were down at Everblades Arena. Sheldon wasn't playing that particular game and he was sitting in the stands watching with Frost and some kind of an argument broke out. And you see Frost just ripping him, ordering him to 'get away from here' and I was watching Sheldon not leaving as Frost yelled 'get out of here.' It was like watching an abusive parent or something with a kid who didn't want to leave. And finally Sheldon is walking down the steps with his head down, almost crying, walking slowly. It was a sad thing to watch."

After an episode like that one, Keefe would be lost for a few days, lost from his teammates, his game out the window. "We'd almost have to pick him up," says Feaster. "But he was a different kid when Frost was around from when he wasn't around. Some days, you'd see Sheldon during our rookie tournament and he was constantly on the phone. Practice couldn't end fast enough. He was on the phone. I don't know who he was talking to, but I suspect it was Frost."

In one of Feaster's conversations with Frost, he told him he wasn't helping Keefe's career.

"I only took his calls out of respect for Sheldon, who I liked," says Feaster. "But I told him flat out, 'You're not helping him.' I'd say to him, 'I have twenty-two other guys on active, forty-six guys in my system, I'm not getting phone calls from any of their agents. Don Meehan or Pat Morris or any of the big agents aren't calling. I shouldn't be getting these from you.' I would never say to him, 'Don't call this number.' I didn't think that was right for Sheldon. But I would say, 'Do you understand, you're not helping

Sheldon? You may think you're helping him but you're not. You're especially not helping his relationship with the head coach because Torts is not the kind of coach who takes well to that kind of thing.' We didn't appreciate the constant harassment over one player, and that's what it was. Maybe harassment is too strong a word for what it was, but it was a constant drumbeat on how we were misusing Sheldon.

"And it wasn't just Frost. Tortorella told me a story once that they were playing Jersey and Danton skated by the bench and yelled something at Torts. Now that kind of jawing back and forth happens all the time. But this was completely different. He wasn't yelling something abusive at him—he yelled something about Sheldon and the way Torts was treating him. Can you imagine being on a bench and hearing something like that? That's how twisted this whole thing was."

But the coaches and management liked Sheldon Keefe, just as Danton liked him. They thought he was fine young man, if perhaps a bit misguided, and had a promising future. But even kids the coaches like, even kids with a future, have to pay their dues in the minors sometimes.

And, like Danton, Keefe wouldn't do that.

"Sheldon was a very good AHL player, but when he came up to play in the NHL," says Feaster, "he just didn't have enough. We wanted him to develop more at the AHL level. He didn't want to play in the minors. He wasn't willing to invest in his career. And it didn't help that someone was always telling him he was being used improperly."

In each of his three years in Tampa, he split seasons between the NHL Lightning and their AHL and IHL affiliates. But unlike many young players, who accept minor-league assignments with the hope they can work their way back to the big leagues, Keefe never accepted his demotions well. He always thought he was too good for the AHL.

A few years ago, Feaster and Lou Lamoriello happened to start a conversation when the topic turned to Danton and Keefe. They started swapping stories. They talked about the phone calls. They talked about the unwillingness to play in the AHL. They talked about the layers of co-dependence—Frost with Danton and Danton with Frost; Frost with Keefe and Keefe with Frost.

"Our stories were so similar," says Feaster. "And I remember Mike Gillis sharing with me how incredibly frustrating it was to deal with Danton and Keefe because of Frost's constant involvement."

One more similarity: Keefe was drafted by the Lightning in 1999 and Tampa Bay won the Stanley Cup in 2004. By then, the Lightning had dispatched Keefe to Hershey of the American League, still hoping he might turn out to be an NHL player. Tampa had exposed Keefe on waivers at the beginning of the season, and he was claimed by the New York Rangers. But he never did play a game in New York. He was put on waivers again and reclaimed, oddly by Tampa, who let him go after he played no part in their Stanley Cup–winning season. That summer, he signed with the Phoenix Coyotes, was placed in Utah of the AHL, and lasted only four games with the Grizzlies before coming to the realization his career was going nowhere.

The statistics indicate that Sheldon Keefe scored 12 goals in the 125 NHL games he played for Tampa, which, considering his skill level, branded him a huge disappointment.

"You know what?" says Jay Feaster. "If Sheldon had played his cards right, gone to the minors, developed the way he should have, he probably would have a Stanley Cup ring today."

He can thank Dave Frost for missing out on the championship season that got away—and the career that may have followed.

It's not just Stanley Cup rings that that have slipped through the fingers of those whose lives Dave Frost has touched. Most people manage to live full lives without ever raising the most difficult trophy in team sport to win. What no one can live without is the warmth of friends and family, the people with whom we might share our accomplishments, or turn to for support. And it is precisely these bonds of trust and affection that fray and snap when Frost becomes involved in a family.

On the day after Mike Danton was arrested in 2004, a woman named Irene McCauley phoned the *Toronto Sun* and began to cry.

"Maybe this will bring her home," the widow of the former National Hockey League head of officiating, John McCauley, said into the telephone. "Maybe this is the breakthrough we needed. Maybe this will smarten her up."

She was talking with hope and despair, speaking a few words, crying in between, then speaking some more. Two of Irene McCauley's children figure in the hockey world: Bridget, better known to some as the wife of Dave Frost, and Wes, an NHL referee (just as her husband had been). As a teenager, Bridget left home against her parents' advice, moved in with Frost, and eventually married him. The family was stunned by the development and so dismayed that they had almost no contact at all with Frost over the years. "It's a good thing John isn't around to see this," his wife would say often.

And always, when references were made in print to Frost and his family, she would request to not have her family name mentioned "out of respect for John's good name."

Irene McCauley thought that Danton's arrest, and the attempted murder of Bridget's husband, after all that already had gone on, would bring her daughter home. "I think this is a sign," she said. "This is a chance we've kind of waited for, a chance for Bridget to get out." Like so many of the parents of Frost's hockey-playing boys, Irene believed that her daughter was being held against her will, even if that hasn't been proven true over time.

As a mother she was afraid for her daughter, afraid of Frost. And like so many parents who have been involved in his life, she's always been uncertain about what to do to change anything.

"That was a part of Dave I understand the least," says Sue Jefferson. "Now, I understand the hockey part, trying to turn the kids pro and all that. I have a sense of what that is all about. What I don't understand is the apparent pleasure he took from destroying people. Whatever he might have put into those relationships, it didn't help people, it only hurt people. It only divided people. What kind of person does that?"

For much of his adult life, and much of Mike Jefferson's child-hood, Steve Jefferson's best friend was Brian Keefe, Sheldon's father. They met when the kids were young, lived in the same neighbourhood, enjoyed hockey and beer, and beer and hockey, in no particular order. "We became instant best friends," said Steve Jefferson. "I never had to look very far for Brian. He was always at my house, watching whatever hockey game was on that night." The two men would drive to minor-hockey games together, share hotel rooms on the road, play with the kids on the outdoor backyard rink at the Jeffersons' home. When Steve and Sue bought a small cottage in Muskoka, the Keefes would be there on most weekends.

There was at least one difference between the two. Steve Jefferson was a supporter of Frost in the early years. Keefe had his doubts.

"Keefe hated Frost and Frost hated him," says Steve. "Frost's way of dividing people would be to make up stories about them. He used to tell us that Brian beat his wife all the time, but I never saw that. It was nonsense. The only person I saw beaten up was Sheldon and that was after Frost punched him in the mouth. I know Brian never laid a hand on his wife.

"There was a point in time for quite a while that Brian was really ready to kill Frost." But then everything changed when [Sheldon's mother] was cleaning her house one day in 2001 and accidentally she came across some photographs—the shots taken at Frost's cottage during the two weeks Tom Jefferson was all but held hostage.

Those photos found their way into the hands of Dr. Brian Shaw of the NHL Players' Association, then the police and Children's Aid Society. The Keefes wanted to do the right thing. What neither Steve Jefferson nor Brian Keefe saw coming was that the right thing would lead to their own estrangement. Dr. Shaw met with both families in June 2001 at the Keefes' home and informed them he had no choice but to call in the authorities. According to Steve, Dr. Shaw said, "This man [Frost] is a pedophile. He has to be charged."

When the photographs first came to light, Steve Jefferson tried handling things his own way. When he and Sue first saw the photographs, shocking as they may have been, Steve sat at the kitchen table waiting for Mike and his friends to show up. Brian was on his way, too. "I had about eight chairs around the table waiting to see if we couldn't hash out what happened at the cottage with Tom."

Then, in his words, "everything went crazy. Nothing got settled." It seemed everyone had their own agenda in that summertime meeting. The Jeffersons, angry about what had happened to Tom, wanted answers. The Keefes, realizing the legal and personal can of worms that had been opened here, began backpedalling, protecting their son. Sheldon was furious with his parents for what he believed was breaching his privacy. Mike was furious with his parents for exposing Frost to more scrutiny. Fingers were pointed in all directions and it was clear the Jeffersons wanted to pursue the matter legally and the Keefes were suddenly second-guessing their position of sharing the gruesome photos with the authorities. Steve tried to talk to Mike and his friends—more than talk, almost bully them—to find out what happened, or more specifically, to get them to tell him what exactly went on. But it all ended quickly in a loud argument. What Steve had hoped would be a civil way of addressing a serious problem ended in total and life-altering chaos.

A few days later, Brian Keefe came over to the house to talk.

"My old lady is pissed at you," he said.

And Steve said, "Too bad for your old lady. Tell her to mind her own business."

"You stirred up all this shit with the pictures and everything," Brian Keefe said. "It's causing big trouble." By then, the police were involved and not only was Frost being asked questions, but so were many of his players, including Sheldon Keefe.

And that marked the end of the Jefferson–Keefe friendship. Sheldon turned against his parents, blaming them for turning over private photographs to the Jeffersons, and by extension to Shaw, the police, and other agencies.

Sheldon had a threat for his parents that the Jeffersons knew all too well: "If you want anything to do with me, you'll have nothing to do with the Jeffersons." It was no different with his younger brother, Adam, a budding Frost acolyte who wanted his parents to steer clear of the Jeffersons.

"I'm not allowed to talk to you any more," Brian Keefe said. "The only way I'm going to see my boys is if I wash my hands of you.... Otherwise, the kids won't ever talk to me again."

"Brian walked out of my house that day, with a dozen beer bottles in a twelve-pack, and as he left, he fired it against the brick wall and the bottles smashed all over the place. That was basically the end of our relationship."

Steve Jefferson and Brian Keefe see each other on occasion but only circumstantially. They are no longer friends.

"They [the Keefes] have never wanted to speak out about what happened," said Sue Jefferson. "They don't want to be like us. Everybody had their little things they don't want the public to know about and when it mattered most, they shut up. I'm disappointed in them, to be honest. Disappointed and saddened. We had many years of a great friendship. In a sad way, I understand what they did. They did it to save their own kids, so they could see their kids, have some kind of relationship. But they had to end one relationship to keep another. The whole thing makes me sad."

Sue Jefferson says they didn't see the big picture in the earlier days. The longer they've had to sit back as a family and figure out all that's gone wrong, the more perspective they have gained.

Back in the winter of 1996, she realizes, long before Mike Jefferson changed his name and left his family behind, Sue missed a clear sign of how Frost dealt with families when they weren't around.

It came in a hospital room after a Quinte Hawks game. Larry Barron, who had spent time living in their home and had been something of a mentor to Mike as an older member of the team, had been badly injured. In the words of Steve Jefferson, he had "thrown himself" in front of a puck, all but shattering his jaw. He was rushed to emergency, and the Jeffersons came along in support.

Barron's mouth was immobilized and threaded with tubes. Because the player couldn't talk, Frost spoke for him. When Frost was asked about Larry's family, his answer bewildered the Jeffersons. "He has none."

"I'm there thinking his parents are in Brampton somewhere, I've seen them," says Sue Jefferson.

Years later, she thought about it a lot.

"Who sets out to destroy families?" Sue asks. "Who thinks this way?"

Like some of Frost's other players, Barron has something to show for all he lost. His season with the Hawks was his last as a competitive hockey player, but he has managed to parlay his knowledge of the game into a career as an instructor at his own Barron Hockey Academy in California. Still, his name will always be bound up with Frost's.

In part, that is because Frost has appropriated Barron's name— and more than once. *The Globe and Mail* reported in May 2004 that Frost masqueraded as Barron in conversations with veteran hockey columnist David Shoalts over a two-year period dating back to September 2001. Posing as Barron, he would promise exclusive interviews with the *Globe* about the Jeffersons, the police investigations focused on him, and other details about this most unusual hockey story—and then not deliver on the promises. "Mike thinks Dave is his father," Frost, pretending to be Barron, had told Shoalts. "He thinks the world of him.... This guy saved the kid's life."

Shoalts firmly believed he was speaking with Barron and didn't discover he had been duped until he heard Frost interviewed on *The Bill Watters Show* on what was then MOJO Radio in Toronto in May 2004. He heard the voice and instantly identified the man he had been talking to for years. Seeking an explanation, he left voice-mail messages for both Frost and Barron. Neither called back. Instead, bizarrely, Sheldon Keefe returned the call. Or, as Shoalts wrote in the *Globe*, at least he said he was Keefe.

During the radio interview with Frost on Watters's program, which exposed Frost in Shoalts's mind, Frost said, "This kid is like a son to me ... it goes far beyond a player–agent relationship. I'm like a father figure to him."

In early 2003, Frost (posing as Barron) told Shoalts that they should write a book together, one that every hockey parent in North America would want to read. "How parental greed and abuse tore apart a young man's life."

That book, of course, was never written. Barron, for public consumption, wants nothing to do with Frost any more. Whether they now have a relationship or not is impossible to know. Barron once lived in Frost's home in Brampton and also with the Jefferson family. He refused to be interviewed on the subject.

When you survey the landscape of Frost's hockey relationships, it is not unlike arriving at a house fire too late: All that's left are memories and ashes.

Just ask Gord Smith, a police officer familiar with Frost, the Jeffersons, and the minor-hockey scene in and around Brampton. "I bet they all live a pretty lonely life," he says of those who became entangled in Frost's web. "I bet the only friends they have is themselves. Dave preyed on weak kids from troubled homes. He took a lot of low-income kids from Brampton and turned them against their families."

After all these years, Sue Jefferson wishes she understood it all better.

"I don't know what happened with these kids or these families, but it can't be a coincidence," says Sue Jefferson. "Look at all the relationships ruined. There's a thread here connecting everyone. We've all been punished in a way for having Dave Frost in our lives.

"Steve lost his son and his best friend. Everybody lost something. That's how Dave works. He separates you from everyone you love. That's the power for him. He takes those things away from people. All to keep a secret of some kind—inappropriate behaviour of some kind—with him, it's physical, it's mental. It's funny, back in the beginning when Dave used to talk to Steve a lot on the phone, we would joke about him being a puppet master. We would joke about it and then we saw those same words written in the paper. We don't joke about it much any more."

Dear Mike

It has been a long time since I wrote you. I miss you so much it is literally killing me. This whole ordeal has put so much stress on our family I don't know where it will end.... I am trying to reach out to you. Please accept my hand. I can't even begin to understand what you have gone through the last four years. Apparently you will be coming back to Canada soon. Please don't ever feel that you can't come home, even for a visit.

I accept full blame for what ... (lines missing)

Please contact your mom and brother, even if you don't want to talk to me, even if you hate me and I pray you don't, the healing has to begin.

I believe that it would probably be the hardest moment of your life to show up at our doorstep, but only for the first moment. There is an old saying that love means never having to say you are sorry and God that is so true ...

Mike, I know that you fear seeing me more than anyone else because I am your father. I know that because I had a father and he's gone and I miss him almost as much as I miss you.

Fathers are very forgiving, understanding. Believe me, all you have ever done is make me proud.

I wish I had held up my end of the bargain. Tom and I had a big blow-up tonight. I worry about him.

It truly sucks that so many people can be affected by one person. Mike, please take the time to read this letter. I took the time to write it.

Love Dad

[The letter was torn into little pieces; some of the pieces were not returned in the envelope.]

12

The People vs. David Frost

The case against David Frost was lost before it ever really began.

August 22, 2006, was a rare day of celebration for the Jefferson family—the day Frost was charged by the Ontario Provincial Police with twelve counts of sexual exploitation. Finally, it seemed, the truth would come out. Justice would be served. Their son was already estranged and behind bars, his brief playing career already snuffed out. Their lives remained in turmoil, scarred forever. To see Frost prosecuted for even a fraction of what he had done might not change the past. But it could bring some small measure of justice. And justice was something they still believed in.

"We've been waiting so long for this," Steve Jefferson said at the time, after Frost was taken into custody. A long time indeed. The OPP were trying to settle accounts from nearly a decade earlier, when Frost made his move to the outlaw Metro Junior Hockey League and took his chosen players. That was back in 1996–97, the one season the Quinte Hawks played in Napanee. That was before any of the Frost trades that saw his acolytes moved around the OHL, before the Barrie Colts embarrassed themselves at the

Memorial Cup. It was long before Jefferson was ever drafted, before Tom Jefferson spent a harrowing two weeks at Frost's cottage in 2000. Ancient history, but something that had to be addressed. And the Jeffersons would take justice where they could get it.

"I can't believe it has finally happened," said Steve Jefferson. "I'm going to go home and tell my wife. And she's going to bawl her eyes out."

Those were tears of happiness. There haven't been many since.

Things looked good for the prosecution when the charges were laid. Police investigators believed they could count on a slam-dunk, sure-thing conviction. To get a guilty conviction in a sexual-exploitation case, the prosecution must show that the accused has authority over a young person and exploits him or her for sexual purposes. And there were more than a few people who knew David Frost and who figured that was a pretty fair description of the way he did business.

The Jefferson family had little doubt about Frost's guilt. They believe Frost should have been charged for his alleged abuse of Tom during his fortnight at Frost's cottage. The investigating officers from the OPP felt exactly the same way. To this day, many people are angry about the fact that Frost walked away from his trial unscathed, but they don't want to talk about it on the record. They thought they had Frost once. They were well aware of his practices. They knew who he was and had a pretty good idea of what he was up to. They wanted him. They wanted him badly. And when they began the second investigation of Frost, the sexual-exploitation case, the OPP went at it hard.

They spent two and a half years, at a significant cost, investigating Frost. The criminal investigation had a narrow focus: Frost's living arrangements and all that went on during the one sordid Quinte Hawks season (1996–97) that has been the focus of much media attention. Frost lived in Room 22 of the Bay View Inn, an ordinary motel in the tiny town of Deseronto, Ontario. The twenty-nine-year-old coach shared the two-bedroom suite with three young players—one as young as sixteen; two of them twenty—and it wasn't unusual for the coach, the players, and their girlfriends to drink and party on any given night.

What went on in that motel was not a mystery to anyone involved by 2006. There was a lot of sex—and a lot of sex many in the courtroom found disgusting and troubling. The question, though, was whether it was a crime. That is, did Frost use his position of authority as hockey coach to orchestrate sexual acts that involved his players, their girlfriends, and himself? Would the prosecution be able to establish, beyond a reasonable doubt, that it was Frost's control over these young men that led to the sexual acts?

But anyone hoping for justice when charges were laid in 2006 had a long wait and a number of disappointments in store before the case even came to trial. There were problems with the case, and they had little to do with the facts and much to do with external politics. The number of charges against Frost dropped from twelve to four. Almost all of the difficulties related to the case were out of the hands of the OPP and the team of investigating officers.

For reasons never entirely explained by anyone in authority, the disturbing case against Frost turned into a legal game of political hot potato as it was passed from Crown attorney to Crown attorney. No one seemed willing to take it on, and if someone did, the person didn't last very long in the job.

What appears to have dogged the prosecution's case is a letter written by one of the first Crowns assigned to the case, Lee Burgess of Belleville, Ontario. Burgess had expressed to all parties involved that he believed a conviction would be unlikely. Not long after writing the letter, Burgess was pulled from the case in November of 2007 by a senior Crown in Toronto named Ken Campbell. He took the case out of eastern Ontario and into the head office in Toronto. Campbell wasn't about to give up that easily—but the residue of Burgess being removed from the case remained.

Campbell then assigned the case to two other Crowns: Kenneth Anthony and Alex Smith, who had Burgess's work on the matter and were asked to determine whether the case should, in fact, go forward. Clearly, there was disagreement among prosecutors, and Campbell was adamant the case wouldn't fall through the cracks of a busy justice system. While the Frost affair may not have been a Toronto matter, the case landed at 720 Bay Street, which, in police vernacular, is where major decisions are made by the Attorney General of Ontario's office in downtown Toronto. Campbell didn't want this high-profile case buried and, after doing their due diligence, Anthony and Smith believed it should proceed as well.

Whether any of the Bay Street machinations played a part in the endgame of the case is debatable, but it may have mattered to Judge Geoffrey Griffin in Napanee. Small towns in Ontario don't care much for Toronto politics, in court or in other venues. And while Judge Griffin clearly enjoyed the national media attention that went along with the case—he is a character who enjoys his unique sense of humour, which on occasion would cross the line of good taste—he may not have appreciated the delays or that key decisions were being made in the big city a two-hour drive away.

Finally, at a May 2008 pretrial motion hearing, Judge Griffin took the prosecution to task.

Almost two years after charges had been laid, the case had yet to go to trial. Judge Griffin considered throwing out the case, citing the excessive delays, and castigated the Crown for its "I-don't-want-it, you-take-it" attitude.

"I've never been involved in a case that took so long to deter-mine whether there was a reasonable possibility of conviction," Judge Griffin said to a near-empty courtroom.

"If Mr. Frost isn't frustrated, I am frustrated. You're allowed to frustrate judges," said Griffin, pointing at the prosecutor of the day, Jay Naster, who was about to pass the Frost file on to its seventh or eighth attorney.

"You're lucky I'm not cynical," said Griffin pointing, smiling wryly. "There is a revolving door of Crowns. No one will accept responsibility for the case. I am ... surprised at the rotated Crown phenomena. I've got Crowns who say, 'I'm here today, gone tomorrow.'

"My sense is that the integrity of the process has been comprom-ised.... We have a lot of cases where we see a lot of monkeys, but don't see a lot of organ grinders."

Eventually, Griffin would rule that the case would proceed—and finally, the prosecution's game of musical chairs slowed to a halt. The case was assigned to Toronto Crown Sandy Tse, a well-regarded office lawyer not known for high-profile work in criminal court. As a quiet, low-profile prosecutor, Tse was a strange choice to handle a high-profile case. But people in the Toronto office of the Crown attorney—the big city had taken over this wayward case, and they wanted one of their own handling it, even if the person was a bad fit for the job at hand.

Dave Frost always said the truth would come out. That has been a standard line of his for as long as he has been in trouble. Ask him a question about any of the controversial aspects of his life and you will hear that answer. He won't tell you the truth—he'll just promise that one day it will come out.

In the case against Frost, the truth did come out, in troubling and at times sensational testimony, in a court case that seemed to have everything backwards right from the beginning. That was just part of the trouble. Never mind the game of musical chairs played by the prosecution that led up to the trial. In this bizarre and murky case, up seemed down, down seemed up, and the abnormal seemed to sub in for normal. The two alleged victims of Frost's crime were former junior-hockey players he coached and mentored. Normally, the victims testify for the prosecution. In fact, the prosecution is working *on behalf of* the victims. But not in that Napanee courtroom. In this case, the victims testified for the defence. But that wasn't all.

The two former players, teenagers when they were involved with Frost in Deseronto, were full-grown adults on the witness stand. But the law dictated that their identities be protected under a publication ban since they were minors at the time of the alleged offence. Because they were deemed victims by the court, even if they were testifying *for* Frost, the former hockey players were entitled to the protection of the law.

Testifying for the prosecution were the boys' ex-girlfriends, and they expected to have their names protected as well. In fact, the ex-girlfriends had agreed to come forward to tell their wild and sordid stories based on the promise that their names would not be publicized. But they didn't find out until the case had begun that they would not be afforded the same protection as the hockey players, who were pitting their testimony against that of the ex-girlfriends. For legal purposes, they were considered witnesses, not victims.

In listening to their heart-rending testimony, it was impossible for spectators not to see that these girls had been victims in some important sense. But under the strict definition of the charges, it was not the ex-girlfriends whom Frost was accused of exploiting. And so, in the end, the court ruled that the men's identities would remain private but the women's would not. This injustice hung over the trial like a poisonous fog.

On the witness stand, the two women spoke with brutal and disturbing honesty of their sexual involvement with their boyfriends and with Frost. That their names were being disclosed by some publications (some media outlets chose not to use their names) only added to the difficulty they faced and the personal humiliation of divulging stories of their past and acts they were clearly embarrassed by.

One of the star Crown witnesses, a young woman named Karen (not her real name), testified in court that she lost her virginity to her hockey-playing boyfriend on New Year's Eve that season. She was, she told the court, a shy sixteen-year-old girl at the time— sexually inexperienced, unsure of herself, terribly introverted, but smitten with her boyfriend, one of the new players that had set Deseronto abuzz. Karen's story of her first sexual encounter, and her ability to hold up under questioning despite her obvious shyness, was stirring yet believable.

Then her testimony turned to Frost.

Just months after her first sexual experience, and mere days after engaging in sex for the very first time, Karen testified that she was coerced into a threesome by her boyfriend, who cannot be identified. She admitted to agreeing reluctantly.

"I thought it was going to be Mike [Danton]," she testified about the third participant in the threesome. "I was shocked that it was him [Frost].... I didn't want him."

Frost was twenty-nine years old at the time. Karen was sixteen. Her boyfriend had just turned sixteen.

"Both men starting kissing me," Karen testified about being in the bedroom of Frost's motel suite. She spoke so quietly her troubling testimony was barely audible. "[My boyfriend] was the first to have sex with me…. I was laying on top of Dave while this was happening. He asked if I wanted him to go faster or slower. I didn't want to answer…. I don't know how long it lasted … I've always been uncomfortable with that because I was forced into it."

This was one of the moments—one of the many—that the Jeffersons believed Tse failed to capitalize on in court, both emotionally and legally. Karen's testimony was powerful and rang of truth. It was one thing for a young, shy, uncertain girl to have sex with her boyfriend for the very first time. It may not have been a decision she would make again, but that's the kind of thing kids do. It was another matter entirely for this nervous girl to be pushed again so quickly to do something she clearly wanted no part of. This happened not once, but twice, she testified. That it took place in the coach's bedroom of the motel suite, with the coach participating, could have been something the trial turned on.

Frost's attorney, Marie Henein, denied that her client had had any involvement in threesomes or other sexual activities with the young players or girls. "But why would a young woman, twelve years removed from the alleged crime, with her name made public, with only embarrassment coming her way, have a reason to lie?" asked Sue Jefferson. The very fact that this young woman was willing to show up, with much to lose and nothing to gain but a sense of justice, should have given her the benefit of the doubt that the defence managed to conjure. And it nearly did hold sway in the courtroom. Her wrenching testimony left little sympathy for the former Quinte Hawks coach.

But the prosecution had more witnesses to call, and more work to do. And not all of them could convince the court the way Karen did. Nor did Tse seem up to the challenge of wringing from his witnesses the kind of testimony he needed to prove not only that sordid things had happened under Frost's watch, but also that they were the direct result of Frost's influence and manipulations.

The prosecution had much of its hopes pinned on Hawks assistant captain Ian LaRocque. He knew what had gone on, was supposed to be one of the prosecution's star witnesses, and was there to tell the truth. Frost kept saying the truth would come out, even if he wasn't about to divulge it. Now LaRocque had travelled from Texas to make sure it did.

But it didn't work out that way at all.

Somehow, as LaRocque painted a picture of tawdry group sex, it came to seem quite normal, not at all something for which David Frost was uniquely to blame. LaRocque testified that within hockey culture, threesomes and foursomes were not at all unusual. It wasn't, he said, the least bit unusual for one girl to have sex with two or three boys at a time. He said it happened on many of the teams he was involved with. He had travelled all that way to make clear how abnormal the goings-on at the Bay View Inn had been. But his lopsided testimony made the group sex sound like the normal life of a puck bunny.

Veteran court reporters covering the trial were astonished again and again by the questions that were not asked:

Did any of those sexual encounters take place in your coach's home, with your coach participating?

Was your coach aware of such encounters?

Was your coach naked in a bedroom with teenaged girls and boys from any other team, in any other place?

Did your coach orchestrate any of these encounters?

When the moment came to pry open the wormy can of Frost's involvement in the various orgies, the questions never came. Not one of them. Afterwards, Donald Dickson, LaRocque's attorney, was terribly unhappy and frustrated. He complained about the prosecution. He complained about what a waste of time it was to fly up here with his client from Texas only to realize the Crown was not going to ask any of the questions they had come to answer. They weren't there to talk about hockey in general—they were there to talk about what was so troublingly *different* about the daily environment surrounding the Hawks.

The prosecution and the OPP, meanwhile, were just as frustrated by LaRocque's performance in court, claiming afterwards that whatever it was he had told police in his interviews with them, he did not repeat for the courts. But LaRocque maintained that he could only answer the questions he was asked. He wasn't there to deliver a lecture.

"I had so much more I wanted to say," LaRocque said back at the Hampton Inn Hotel after his testimony ended. "They didn't ask the right questions. They didn't ask me anything I expected to be asked."

Whether the prosecution or the witness was to blame was immaterial. The failure to communicate only played into Henein's brilliant defence. All she had to do was prove reasonable doubt. And if there was one thing the police, the Crown, and their own witnesses managed to communicate, it was uncertainty.

It was Tse's job, on the other hand, to take the testimony and the facts, all of which left no doubt that something wretched and wrong had happened in that threadbare motel room over several months, and galvanize that moral outrage into certainty that what had happened was a crime. Tse needed to probe, to ask questions about hockey, about sex and power and the culture of intimidation and conformity. Basic questions that he failed to ask, failed to follow up on. Questions that might have turned the case in the prosecution's favour.

Many who were watching from the courtroom seats were incredulous and sickened. Sue Jefferson sat through every day of the case, hearing stories no mother should ever hear, growing frustrated with a case she knew was slipping away. She already felt a lingering disgust for a justice system that failed to bring Tom's case to trial. That disgust only grew as she watched the case against Frost unravel before her eyes.

"I don't know much about courts, but the worst part of the legal system for me is seeing a high-quality defence attorney and a mediocre prosecutor," she said. "It's not a fair fight. Sitting through the trial wasn't nice. No mother wants to hear this, but there were all kinds of questions I wanted to ask that never got asked. And what I don't understand is, if a person like me had these questions, how come the lawyer didn't ask them?"

Frost's alleged involvement in threesomes was disclosed to the court perhaps most powerfully in a diary kept by the young Karen. In the diary, she noted the dates she had sex with her boyfriend, and how many times they engaged in each encounter. When asked in court what the notation "three times minus one" meant, she answered softly, "I didn't want to count Dave."

She counted it, then subtracted.

When asked what else they did in Frost's room at the Bay View Inn, Karen answered that she "watched hockey games and had a lot of sex."

Karen testified that she twice was involved in threesomes that included her boyfriend and Frost. When asked to recall the sex with Frost, Karen winced, "He was shaved," she said of Frost's pubic area. "It irritated me."

But the issue wasn't whether Frost participated in threesomes. Whatever the court thought of that behaviour, at least it wasn't illegal in itself. The question was whether Frost had used his authority and influence to orchestrate some of that sex. Karen clearly indicated how the players had been instructed by their coach, not only on the ice, but also in bed. The players were even told what sexual positions to try. Karen testified that "he [Frost] would come in [to the bedroom] and help [us] do the top position when [her boyfriend] was ready."

If that is not "influence," it is difficult to imagine what is.

"I didn't want him to [be there]," Karen testified. "I guess I was shocked by it." But she never said anything to protest. That bothered her then; it bothers her now. She didn't want to jeopardize her relationship, and the defence preyed on that. The girls, Henein insisted, were willing to do anything to maintain their relationships with the budding hockey stars. Anything.

Karen said she didn't protest her boyfriend's wishes and Frost's involvement "because I was the quiet one," and she had figured out if she wanted to keep seeing her boyfriend, she needed Frost's approval. Because *he* needed Frost's approval. If Frost didn't accept her, she was out.

Near the end of her testimony, Henein attacked Karen with cool, ruthless efficiency: "We know there were threesomes with Mr. Frost in Deseronto … because you say so?" she asked, her question dripping with dramatic sarcasm.

But the uncomfortable Karen, obviously vulnerable and on the verge of tears, held her own for that moment and answered sharply, "Because I *know* so."

That was one of the few times in the trial that Henein was on her heels. Maybe the only time. Henein wasn't just an attorney in this case—she was the orchestra conductor, always in charge of her players. She was the mesmerizing scene-stealer. If the courtroom battle between Marie Henein and Sandy Tse had been a boxing match, the referee might have stopped the contest partway through the trial. It was that much of a mismatch. Henein is bright, quick, formidable, and sure of herself. She was meticulously organized, quick to pick up on any inconsistency, and she took clear advantage of every opportunity to question and undermine the prosecution's case against Frost.

Piece by piece, Henein dismantled even the most credible of witnesses. She didn't have to alter the facts themselves or even make things black and white. But in each case, she managed to plant all kinds of seeds of reasonable doubt or suspicion.

Tse was almost the complete opposite in court. Lacking personality and presence as a courtroom orator, Tse seemed out of his element. Perhaps he is a superb lawyer behind a desk. Perhaps he understood what he was up against in the case from a legal perspective, but he failed to understand what had gone on in Room 22 of the Bay View Inn or how the Hawks team was run by Frost. He didn't seem to understand the social dynamic, or feel the human cost—and he certainly didn't seem to understand the culture of the game. There is a "line up and do what you're told" attitude that permeates hockey at all levels and Tse never explored that. It is a game that expects and demands conformity, even in some cases when that conformity means breaking the law or certainly stepping outside the bounds of good taste. Hockey players, like athletes in many sports, especially team sports and contact sports that foster a warrior mentality, are not invited to think for themselves or question the authority of the coach or the group.

There should have been no doubt at all that David Frost exerted immense influence over his players—that should have been a given even before any allegations arose. So Frost could never have been just another guy partying with a bunch of underage hockey players and a clutch of teenaged girls. He could *only* have been their leader.

"It was clear he didn't understand the culture of hockey," says Steve Jefferson, who watched much of the court proceedings, sometimes with his wife and sometimes without. Most days, Sue Jefferson would be in attendance in Napanee, sometimes with son Tom at her side. "I still don't understand why they would have assigned him [Tse] to the case," Steve laments. "Really, there were so many questions we kept waiting for him to ask. We would sit there and ask, 'Why isn't he asking this?' or 'Why isn't he challenging that?' I know it drove Sue crazy. She'd call me on the days I wasn't there and she was exasperated by what she was seeing."

From his seat in the fourth row of the courtroom, sitting beside his mother, Tom Jefferson admitted his mind often wandered. He had trouble focusing on all the testimony of the many witnesses, and certainly on many of the legal arguments. He was there to support his family, even if he didn't care to hear from or see any of the old Frost boys he had trouble with in the past.

Tom found himself staring at Frost throughout. He couldn't stop staring. "He looked so guilty," said Tom. "As I sat there, I kept thinking how disgusting he looks. Honestly, I wanted to go over there and kick him in the back of the head and beat the living shit out of him until he wasn't breathing. That's no lie. That's what I was thinking. And really, that's what I thought about on the days I was there."

Sue Jefferson sat through almost every hour of the case, not easily. "For most of it, I was sure we were going to win," she says. "I believed that. It was important for me to be there. I felt I was there, representing Mike. I knew Mike wasn't going to come out of [prison] and point the finger at Dave. Mike needed help. He needed the legal system to help him. And I think the courts let Mike down more than any of us.

"I don't know really what happened, but as the trial went on, I think the judge changed. I didn't like that he seemed buddy-buddy at times with Frost, calling him Frosty. I didn't think that was right. You'd see him laughing and winking at him—I didn't like that either. And I thought he made some rude comments some days. And one day at break, I hear Dave going on to his lawyer about the judge being tainted. And he was really hot about it. His voice was getting loud and he said we need a new judge. I don't know what happened from that time on, but for some reason, it seemed like the judge favoured Dave.

The second of the Crown's star witnesses, a girl named Jackie (not her real name), was less convincing than Karen because she seemed such a willing participant in a variety of sexual activities over quite a lengthy period of time. In the end, Henein poked too many holes in her testimony—she found too many discrepancies between what Jackie had told police on a number of occasions and what she testified to in court not to have established a form of reasonable doubt about any exploitation that may have involved her boyfriend, as victim, and her, as participant.

However, one particular court document—an email Jackie sent to a friend after a threesome involving Frost and her boyfriend—revealed that even this young girl's apparent willingness was the result of a campaign of emotional coercion:

Last night when I was sleeping Dave came and woke me up and said why dont you wanna make [her boyfriend] happy? Then I'm like whatta mean? Then he goes you can make him happy by letting me fuck you then he will fuck you. Then I said if that is the only way he will not be a price any more than fuck him. SO dave left and then they both came back to the room. Then [her boyfriend] asked me and I said no then he kept bugging me finally I said I do not care. So i just laid there. [Her boyfriend] tried to kiss me and stuff but I kept pushing him away. They both just fucked me then left me then left the room. I started crying my eyes out. How bad was I used last night? Then when [her boyfriend] came in to go to bed I was still crying so I got up to go downstairs. He asked what was wrong. I said it does not matter how I feel as long as YOUR happy.

Jackie testified about the first time she had sex with her boyfriend and Frost at the same time. "Dave got on top of me," she said. "He asked [her boyfriend] to help him insert his penis. I could feel [his] hands on [Frost's] penis, kind of playing with it.

"I could feel he was taking Dave's penis and he was rubbing it against me. And then I could feel him put it inside me."

Jackie testified that Frost eventually withdrew his penis and masturbated himself to orgasm. She also testified that her boyfriend was nervous throughout. "He was not himself," she said. "It was almost like he didn't know what he was to do next, like he was waiting for direction."

When it was her boyfriend's turn to enter her, the player apparently had difficulty getting an erection. "Dave was telling him he was a wimp. Dave grabbed him and said, 'Why can't you get hard?'

It was like he was making fun. He grabbed his penis and began tugging on it, saying, 'Come on, you can make it hard.'"

The details of Jackie's testimony were upsetting and disturbing, even if Henein continued to find inconsistencies in her words. But the trial may have turned on a question-and-answer session, when Jackie was asked about an interview she had done with the police. Henein asked her if she told police whether Mr. Frost had any distinguishing features. Jackie had told the officer the same thing she told the court—that he had none.

But a doctor would later testify that Frost had a physical impairment, that at the time he was living in the roadside motel in Deseronto he had been diagnosed as having a plum-sized blood sac that would have resembled a third testicle. The court was stunned to hear the grotesque description.

Jackie had testified that she had performed oral sex on Frost on a number of occasions and had been involved in sex acts with him in the same room. Jackie claimed to have been disgusted by the involvement of Frost in many of her sexual escapades. If this was indeed the case, Henein asked, how could she not have noticed such a deformity?

Yet on this issue, again, Tse missed an opportunity to salvage an important piece of evidence. He never asked a simple question—whether her eyes were open or closed when these acts took place.

In his eventual ruling of not guilty, after days of testimony, Judge Griffin said he found the testimony of both young women to be inconsistent. He accused them of collusion, while at the same time accusing Frost's former players of going to any lengths to protect their old coach. For whatever reason, Griffin concluded that even if both sides happened to be stretching the truth somewhat—and it was clear that some of the boys perjured themselves on the witness stand—the Crown had not fulfilled its burden of proof.

Despite everything the court had heard, Frost was going to walk.

Legally, Griffin made the only ruling possible. But that is a long way from saying Frost was fully exonerated.

While making his ruling, Griffin took a swipe at the prosecution. He called out the Crown for not making its case as complete as it should have been. Griffin wondered why Frost's infamous control over his boys was never properly illustrated in court. Where were the parents of the hockey players, he wondered, some of whom, including Sheldon Keefe's parents, were on the witness list?

Why weren't they called to the stand?

Judge Griffin also wanted to know why no other coaches or expert witnesses were called. Or sports psychologists. And why were no telephone records produced linking Frost to his players in unsavoury ways?

There was a case to be made against Frost, admitted Griffin, but Tse and the Crown had failed to make it. He basically indicated in his decision that the prosecution not only could have produced a conviction, but *should* have produced one.

And after reading his lengthy decision, Judge Griffin declared Frost not guilty on all four counts of sexual exploitation.

After the verdict, Sandy Tse walked out of the courtroom and offered no comment.

One of the other lawyers, who cannot be identified, left the courtroom and announced, "I'm going home to take a long, long bath."

Steve Jefferson raced from the courtroom, down the stairs, and to the adjacent parking lot. He needed to be alone. He needed to get away because he knew what he might do otherwise. He was ready to explode.

Throughout the case, security officers were assigned to the court because of the worry that Steve might attack Frost. He didn't. He had controlled himself. But he could no longer hold back his disdain for the process.

"It makes me sick," he said. "The Crown let us down. I can't fucking believe this. I guess this proves that money can buy you a ticket out of jail. This is a total disgrace. The Crown was pathetic. They screwed it up. I don't know how the judge can sleep at night."

A few years later, he doesn't feel any differently: "There's no way those young girls, spilling their guts out like that, were lying. There's no way," he said. "Dave always said the truth would come out. The truth came out in court and it didn't convict him. I know in his mind, and in his boys' minds, he won. But in my mind, he lost, no matter what. In the court of public opinion, he lost.

"Ask anyone what they think of Frost. You can't tell me he won that case. He came out of the case a loser. But he should have gone to jail."

And as Judge Griffin finished reading his ruling in court, a sister of one of the star witnesses for the prosecution looked over at Frost in his defendant's chair and said, "Scumball … that's for my sister."

From his courtroom seat, suddenly a free man, Frost turned to the woman and said, with his trademark aplomb and grace, "Go fuck yourself."

October 31, 2005

Dear Mike

Remember the birthday cakes I would make for you? The parties with all your friends? The presents? Where did all the years go? It's been a long time since I have given you a birthday hug. I hope that I don't have to wait too much longer for another one. I hope that you can make something special of your day. Happy 25th Mike. I miss you. Keep your chin up. Things will get better. Always thinking of you. Love Mom. xxoo

Hey Mike, How's it going? I hope you have a good B-day. I'd like to hear from you some day. I'm going through some hard times and need some advice. You know where to find me. Love you Mike.

Tom

[Birthday card sent.]

13

Guilt without Explanation

Upon the conclusion of Criminal Case 04-300049-WDS, *United States of America vs. Michael Sage Danton*, the presiding judge, William D. Stiehl, turned to Danton and said what many others were thinking: "The exact reason or reasons why you felt you had to engage in this murder plot remain a mystery to me," he said. "In over eighteen years on the bench, I have [never] been faced with a case as bizarre as this one."

Even Danton's own lawyer was baffled by the web of lies and obfuscations his client and his client's former agent had spun. "Whatever led him to offer a stranger $10,000 to kill Mr. Frost, and the nature of the compelling relationship that has drawn him back into Mr. Frost's camp, that's his secret," said Danton's attorney, Robert Haar.

Even the court could not untangle the threads of motives and delusions and blunders that led to the mess that Mike Danton made in the spring of 2004 and the crime for which he was about to be sentenced. Together, not even the St. Louis police, the FBI, and a grand jury could confidently connect the dots in such a way that they could explain why Danton had risked so much, and gone to such effort, to have David Frost killed.

But then, *why* was not the biggest question for them.

All they really needed to know was that Danton was guilty, and the hockey player told them so. On July 16, 2004, Danton pleaded guilty to conspiracy to commit interstate murder, a murder for hire attempt in violation of the laws of the state of Missouri. Danton signed a plea agreement that included eleven pages of legalese and another seven pages stipulating the facts of the case. In all, there would be no teary courtroom drama, no shocking public disclosures, no impassioned legal arguments. A guilty plea prevented all that, and kept what Danton's lawyer called his "secrets" safe.

Upon sentencing, Judge Stiehl showed some leniency to Danton, possibly because of his co-operation, and possibly because of the nature of the crime. Stiehl called the plot "poorly devised" and "hapless" and may have let Danton off lightly on the grounds that his attempt at hiring a hit man, as earnest as it may have been, was hardly more dangerous than a prank. He reduced the court fine from the $15,000 expected to just $850. Had Danton gone to trial, he could have faced more than twice the ten-year maximum sentence for the crime. As small as the crime was, the penalty was severe. The prosecution also considered the possibility of additional charges such as obstruction of justice and previous attempts to hire a hit man that would have been added to his sentence. But in the end, Mike Danton co-operated, choosing to avoid a trial, and pleaded guilty to his part in the attempted murder and was sentenced in November 2004 to seven and a half years behind bars.

"Ultimately, this was not about satisfying people's curiosity," Haar said outside the courtroom. "This was about salvaging as much of a young man's life as you can. Life is sometimes messy.

People are complex. There are no simple or satisfying explanations for everything."

There was, in the end, no trial, and so many questions left unanswered. The case of *United States of America vs. Michael Sage Danton* concluded with a signed proclamation of guilt but no real answer as to why.

That was, and is, the chief mystery. Not who the target was: Danton admitted to Frost that he was the target, and had even used a photograph of Frost to identify the target to the hit man. Even Frost had acknowledged that he had been the intended victim, and had already forgiven his protegé. Note how the crime was committed: Danton had left ample incriminating evidence at every turn, and had even unwittingly involved the police well before the "hit" was meant to take place. It wasn't *who*, and it wasn't *how*. The question always was *why*.

The answer remains locked away somewhere in Mike Danton's head.

Why, when Danton finally had what he'd spent his life working for, would he risk it all?

Why, when any other player would be swept up in the adrenaline of the Stanley Cup playoffs, did this player—a competitor who never quit—allow his thoughts to drift toward fantasies of murder?

Even to those who know Mike Danton, it makes no sense. So much of Danton's life, from the time he was fourteen years old, has been beholden to Frost. Frost was everything to him. Surrogate father, mentor, coach, agent, friend, adviser, trainer, conscience. And he was always there, always so close—too close, many believed.

And yet, at this moment, perhaps the worst possible moment, Danton steeled himself to end Frost's life. Not in a split second, not in a moment of murderous frustration, but over several weeks and months. He wanted Frost dead.

Why?

Was it money?

It's clear that Danton owed Frost $25,000, probably from the agent fees due on his contract. Danton hadn't paid the money back, and may not have had it at the time. While it seems economically flimsy to want to pay $10,000 to eliminate a $25,000 debt when you're earning more than $500,000 a year as a professional athlete, that's what Danton told his accomplices he would pay.

The only person who knows the answer to the *why* question may be David Frost himself. In an extraordinary twist, Frost had the chance to ask his client all about it immediately after the botched murder. Danton called Frost almost every day from the Santa Clara Correctional Institute, where he was held until being transferred to St. Louis. And Frost called him, sometimes more than once a day. And every one of their conversations, clandestine as they may have believed them to be, was taped and turned over to the FBI as evidence.

Before a St. Louis judge put a stop to their telephone contact, almost seventeen hours of confusing and manipulative discussion took place, with Frost and Danton inventing stories on the phone, speaking in childlike codes at times, each of them trying to work their way out of a mess they somehow found themselves in.

Like everyone else involved, Frost wanted to know why the young man he'd told the world was like a son to him would want him killed. From behind bars, Danton was unable to answer clearly.

What follows now are edited versions of the FBI tapes: snippets of phone conversations between Danton (speaking from jail) and Frost that tell much of their relationship, including their shady co-dependence. At times, their patter is spoken in a slightly pathetic Abbott and Costello doing "Who's on First?" kind of way:

Frost: Okay. I'm going to say some things to you and we're going to talk a little bit.

Danton: I don't know how much time I have.

Frost: Okay, this is important, Mike. We're going to be careful okay. Who's ah, Pascal Rheaume, what number does he wear again? Don't say it. You know? *[Rheaume was a player on the Blues. He wore the sweater number 25. When Frost asked about "Pascal," he was really asking about whether Danton had told anyone that he owed Frost $25,000.]*

Danton: Yeah.

Frost: When you talked to that girl [Katie Wolfmeyer] that worked over at, you know, where teens go when they don't go to their main rink?

Danton: Yeah.

Frost: Remember that Young Nats coach you had?

Danton: Umm. [Pause ...]

Frost: Talk in a code, Mike. Remember that Young Nats coach you had?

Danton: I'm not catching you.

Frost: Okay. Remember who your Young Nats coach was?

Danton: Ah, yeah.

Frost: Quinte coach?

Danton: Yeah, yeah.

Frost: Did you ever mention that person at all, ah, that name?

Danton: No.

Frost: Did you ever use that figure to anybody, what number does Pascal Rheaume wear, keep that in your head?

Danton: Okay.

Frost: Did you ever use that figure to anybody prior to the other person?

Danton: Use that figure?

Frost: Yeah.

Danton: No.

Frost: Okay, you know right now I won't be mad, right?

Danton: Yeah.

Frost: This isn't the time to talk about being mad. This is support time.

Danton: Right.

Frost: Yeah.

Danton: The figure that Pascal wears.

Frost: Yeah.

Danton: No.

Frost: The suggestion was made by our friend, and he could be fucking with me, but I need to know the answer to give that to the lawyers, okay? Was anybody else ever contacted prior regarding this?

Danton: No.

Frost: C'mon, think hard now.

Danton: We can't be talking in code like this because I'm not catching a lot of things you're saying.

Frost: Okay, Mike, straight out. Did you ever contact anybody else?

Danton: About the number that Pascal wears?

Frost: No, not about the number. Did you ever say, my Young Nats coach, I owe him Pascal. So, I want you to take care of that.

Danton: Can you say that again?

Frost: My Young Nats coach. I owe him Pascal. And I want you to take care of that for me.

Danton: No.

Frost: Because I don't want to pay it.

Danton: No. No.

Frost: Was anybody else besides the place where you don't play games ever contacted regarding the same thing?

Danton: Ah, yeah.

Frost: Okay. Are you sure the number Pascal was never …?

Danton: Yeah.

Frost: You're sure?

Danton: Yeah.

In other words, Danton seems to rule out the possibility that he was motivated by the money owed, even if that is what he told the alleged hit men.

Another theory is that Danton wanted Frost eliminated because his former mentor was in a position to blackmail him. It is true that Frost knew secrets about Danton and all his "boys" that few of them would want disclosed. And apparently Frost had threatened Danton by telling him he was going to go to Blues general manager Larry Pleau and paint him a picture of Danton's carousing, irresponsible lifestyle, and his nights at an East St. Louis strip joint.

But the transcripts of their jailhouse conversations seem to rule out the possibility that Danton was motivated by a desire to escape Frost's threats of blackmail. In fact, Frost seems to rely on Danton to tell him what dirt the Blues might have.

Frost: Any guys on the team know about this kind of stuff?

Danton: What do you mean?

Frost: About how many and this many.

Danton: Umm.

Frost: C'mon Mike, you know that answer.

Danton: Let me look at my sheet.

Frost: Who would it be, R.J.? [Ryan Johnson, his roommate with the St. Louis Blues.] Does R.J. know anything?

Danton: I don't think so. They don't know like how many girls or anything like that.

Frost: So what do they know?

Danton: Uh.

Frost: Want me to just cut to the shit?

Danton: Yeah.

Frost: They're [players] all saying, a lot of them are saying, that you were just like a fucking dog.

Danton: That's what they said. The FBI broad told me that she asked [St. Louis player] Mark Rycroft about me and I said, "What'd he say?" and he said I kept to myself and I was shady. That's why I don't like people knowing too much about my business.

Frost: Did you tell the FBI broad anything?

Danton: That's just what I said.

Frost: Mike, what did we tell you?

Danton: Well it doesn't have anything to do with what went on. She said "I called Mark Rycroft" and I said, "Why did you do that?" She said, "We were trying to find him." I said, "What'd he say?" He said I was quiet.

Frost: Okay, whatever, whatever, whatever.

Danton: Like that's the thing. These guys thought a whole bunch of things but they never really knew anything. Because I wouldn't tell them everything.

Frost: They suggested you jeopardized stuff on game days and stuff. Did you ever do that?

Danton: No.

Frost: Fucking cop bastards lying to me. So you never went to East Sides [a St. Louis strip club] on the day of a game?

Danton: Fucking no.

Frost: Those guys are fucking bastards. Okay, how about did you bang a broad the night before the game?

Danton: No.

Frost: Are you sure? Come on, kid.

Danton: Like 99 percent. Going back and thinking, I don't know but I know that I wouldn't. I know there was times when I could have and I didn't.

Frost: How did you pull this off without talking to me all about it?

Danton: I came over late. I made sure they came over late.

Frost: So there's going to be no secrets from guys on the team come popping up here?

Danton: What do you mean?

Frost: Like anything that's negative for you. Like he doesn't care, like he did drugs.

Danton: No, fucking no.

Frost: Don't get mad at me.

Danton: I'm telling you there's no drugs. The only time I drank was in Nashville.

Frost: Okay. That's cool. So no surprises from the guys? They just think you're a little messed up with broads.

Danton: Probably.

Frost: Okay. They don't know, they just think it.

Danton: Yeah.

"A little messed up with broads" may be a fair enough assessment of Danton's romantic attachments, but it does not provide an explanation for his decision to try to have his mentor murdered.

So both theories—as to why a young man with a golden future in front of him might do something as colossally stupid as ask a near stranger to hire someone she had just met in a bar to plot an assassination—fall apart when it becomes clear what the would-be plotter and the intended victim talk about. It wasn't money. It wasn't blackmail.

So what was it? The clue is not *what* they talked about. It's that they were talking at all.

"Why, if he wanted Dave dead, did he go right back to him?" asks Sue Jefferson. "I thought for a minute this might be a break-through for us. I thought maybe this would bring him home."

That a botched murder attempt would only bring Frost and Danton closer baffles a lot of people. But not Tom Trevelyan, a Peel Regional Police officer and former hockey player. Trevelyan had come to understand the relationship (as much as it can be understood). When the incarcerated Danton turned to Frost first for guidance and advice in prison, it may have shocked others, but it didn't surprise Trevelyan in the least.

"Mike was in prison, alone, scared—who was he supposed to reach out to?" says Trevelyan, who knew the Jefferson family well from both minor hockey and his police work. "It's human nature to reach out to your family—but he was estranged from his birth family. So who was his family? Frost was his family. The other Frost boys were his family. This was the only family he felt he could trust. Once he left his own home, he had nothing else, which is a little sad by itself. He had no one else to turn to. Who would he call? Who would call him?

"I wasn't surprised by this. He had to turn back to the only thing he knew. From the outside, it may not make much sense, but from the inside, understanding the circumstances, it did."

Danton didn't just turn back to his mentor. From behind the prison walls, he all but gave himself back to Frost. He wilted. Remarkably from both a legal and a personal point of view, over the first twelve days Danton spent in the Santa Clara County Jail there were seventy-nine telephone calls between him and the man he apparently wanted dead. The FBI has approximately a thousand minutes of conversation on tape. That is astonishing by almost any standard.

Police assigned to the case, along with the parole judge and the presiding judge, and even the lawyers involved from both sides, have claimed they have never seen or heard of anything like this before. One minute, Danton was trying to have Frost killed; the next minute, it seemed, he was taking his advice. While in prison, Danton was free of Frost, for a while. Free from the controls. Or so it seemed. But within a day of his prison stay, he fell right back into the very control he had apparently plotted so desperately to get away from.

One of Danton's old teammates on the Quinte Hawks would later describe him as "like a dog going to get his master's paper." In a different courtroom, weighing a different crime, Judge Geoffrey Griffin seemed unable or unwilling to accept that David Frost had control over his hockey-playing boys. Throughout that trial, more than four years after the Danton arrest, he openly mocked the prosecution's weak attempts to establish Frost's controlling ways. Perhaps, had he been able to listen to some of the thousand minutes of prison conversation between Danton and Frost, Griffin would have changed his opinion. The tapes are a chilling, revealing portrait of Frost's near-complete control over Danton.

Mike Danton didn't target David Frost over money, or fear for his career. He needed Frost out of his life for the simplest of reasons. He wanted his freedom.

"Maybe this was his one attempt to get away from Frost," says Sue Jefferson, trying to figure out why her son committed the crime that made his assumed name infamous. "Maybe this was his way of trying to end the control."

Mike Kitchen, Danton's last NHL head coach, agrees with Sue Jefferson. "Mike had trouble fitting in on every team he ever played on," says Kitchen. "We were well aware of that, and we monitored him closely because of it. Because of his past and his background, we kept a pretty close eye on him, although in retrospect not close enough. I honestly thought he was starting to make a break-through with [the Blues]. Both as a hockey player and as a person. Everybody knew he was always on the phone all the time, and we never really knew who he was talking to, but we suspected we did. And everybody just thought, 'Well, that's Mike.' But I think he was starting to make a breakthrough with us. He was starting to fit in. And the more he fit in, maybe the less he wanted to make those calls or take those calls."

It would be a cruel irony if Mike Danton felt driven to commit the crime that would ruin his career by the success he had finally found for himself. Had Frost booby-trapped Mike's success? Had he groomed the kid to play the game at the highest level, but left him with so much baggage that when the time came to enjoy and focus on the present, Danton could think of nothing but escaping the past? If so, the only way out was through David Frost.

"Hockey is the kind of sport where guys have to fit together, live together," says Kitchen. "That's what we do. And if you're a role player like Mike, you can't really be an outsider. My understanding was [that] he was an outsider on every team he had played on until he got here [St. Louis]. But he was starting to fit in here. He was making friends. He was standing on his own. He was growing as a person. Maybe that was part of it. Maybe he thought the only way he could continue growing was to do something drastic."

It is difficult not to feel at least a little sympathy for Danton at this point, at the moment he is about to be locked away for years during the prime of his life. For all his misdeeds, all the damage he's caused, all the generous gestures he spurned, his act of self-sabotage makes it clear that the young man who bullied his mother, who dismantled a family, and who tormented grown men on the rinks of the NHL was little more than a confused kid. Someone bewildered by reality. A man with a child's sense of right and wrong, who knew that something had to change, but had no idea how to change it.

Haar described his client as "a knotted ball of emotions." But that may have been only the beginning. Around the time of his arrest, Danton's former lawyer, Michael Edelson, told *The Globe and Mail* that Danton "has been very depressed and possibly suffers from delusions."

It is not necessary, however, to assign a pathological explanation for Danton's poor decisions. The transcripts of Danton's jailhouse conversations with Frost certainly suggest a confused young man with no idea how to twist free of the things that oppress him.

Frost: Why were you even thinking about it then?
Danton: I don't know.
Frost: Well, you've got to tell me…. Just tell me. It's okay.
Danton: It was everything. Just everything. Everything the same. It was just I didn't know. I was just obviously, everything was kind of coming down at the same time.

Frost: Like what?

Danton: Hockey. You know, fighting.

Frost: What month are we talking?

Danton: January maybe. [Note: Danton was arrested in April.]

Frost: Jesus. What happened then?

Danton: Just hockey was going down and fucking everything, all the same shit.

Frost: I don't know what you mean.

Danton: Ah c'mon, read into it, man.

Frost: I know, but Mike, things were never that bad, right?

Danton: I don't know. I just wanted …

Frost: You just wanted what?

Danton: I don't know. I just … fucking, I don't know. I don't know how to say it over here right now.

Frost: Well, try.

Danton: I just wanted, fucking, to do things, you know. And things weren't fucking good between that person and it was like I felt that there was no other way.

This is the rambling of a young man with no idea what to do—someone who simply cannot think straight. This can hardly be surprising to anyone who knows what Danton had gone through in his life. And given that it was Frost, the mentor, the Svengali, who put him through so much during his formative years, it is not much of a stretch to believe, as he says, that "there was no other way." In the upside-down world occupied by Danton and Frost, even the murderous delusions of the bewildered player make a certain sense.

But does that mean Danton was insane? Should anyone take the word of Danton's former lawyer? There is another twist to Danton's psychological state. And, as usual, it involves Frost. It was

Michael Edelson who put Danton in touch with highly regarded St. Louis lawyer Robert Haar. And Edelson had acted in the past for David Frost. In short, it was Frost's lawyer who helped arrange the legal defence of the man accused of attempting to have his client murdered.

Was Frost involved in the defence of the man who wanted him dead? He certainly wanted to be. The transcripts record the pariah coach trying to manage the disgraced player's legal defence over the phone.

Frost: ... Regarding the Young Nats situation, and that picture, that's really bad. Okay? Now what's happened is they're going to try and paint and illustrate what they want. The main lawyer, not the two clowns that are coming there tomorrow, two people coming tomorrow are important because they know the St. Louis district, they know the judge and the prosecutor.

Danton: Okay.

Frost: This is what's being expressed to me. And you know what? I want you to listen and I don't want you to ever think anything different from what I'm about to tell you. Are you ready?

Danton: Yeah.

Frost: It's an absolute impossibility to win this case in the criminal court.

Danton: Okay.

Frost: You'll lose. You'll go seven to ten [years] without question. Okay? That's why, and we know you do need help and there's no question your mental state at the time—you were not thinking clearly. You were on the medications. And so forth, right. Um, your emotional state, tomorrow when you're talking, you need to stay calm. But you have to feel the truth on how you feel.

Danton: Uh huh.

Frost: I'm not saying you have to cry. Can you call me back? Because this is very important. We'll talk right until we get off. Um, so, the only way out is through. Remember I told you there was a medium spot between pleading insanity.

Danton: Uh huh.

Frost: The spot for severe counselling. It's the only way out. Mike, I'm telling you now, it's going to work because you really do need it.

Before Danton was to testify in front of a grand jury in St. Louis, Frost told him what he was to say under oath. FBI Special Agent John Jiminez, the lead investigator in the case against Danton, testified at a bail hearing in St. Louis on May 21, 2004, talking about the prison tapes he had heard.

"In a lot of the calls, Mr. Frost is convincing Mr. Danton that Mr. Danton will get out of jail, that everything will be fine," Jiminez said. "[He promised that he] will be on Mr. Danton's side and will not abandon him and will assist his legal defence in any way so that Mr. Danton can get out of jail. Mr. Frost explains to Mr. Danton that Mr. Danton had to act emotional, like he is insane. Mr. Frost had explained that he, through his association with Bob Goodenow, the NHL Players' Association president, had convinced the Players' Association's Dr. Shaw to come out and see Mr. Danton. And when that happened, Mr. Danton should cry, should act emotional, so that Dr. Shaw would report back that Mr. Danton was having emotional, mental problems."

Those FBI tapes record Frost urging Danton to perjure himself, and then introduce for the first time the absurd red herring that Steve Jefferson, who couldn't possibly have been in Danton's apartment and had never been there, was the target of the murder plot.

Frost: And I'm not going to lie, the negotiation has not gone well so far. So far, their prosecutor, the guy in charge of you—the FBI is not in charge of fuck all, all they do is investigate and give it to the prosecutor—they have no say. The prosecutor is bringing me in on Wednesday, it's called a subpoena, they're going to subpoena me to St. Louis and make me testify before the grand jury.

So I'm going to do that and they're going to say to me, "Did you fight with him?" And I'm going to say no.

"What happened between you?" And I'm going to say the same things that's happened between him and I for ten years. "What'd you talk about?" Talked about the same issues we've always talked about.

"Was there anything big?" Yeah, he had a fucking nightmare Tuesday night after his goal. I walked into his room and he was drenched. He thought Steve Jefferson was in the room with a gun over his head. Those are the things I'm going to say.

They're going to say, "Yeah, you had some sort of fight with him." And I'm going to say, "No I didn't. I had the same thing I've had for ten years. I had a conversation with him about putting his priorities in order and making sure hockey's first."

They're going to try and do what they've been doing the whole thing. They're trying to get me to go south and it's not going to happen and you know it's not. So as long as you understand there's one way and one way only. Okay?

Danton: Uh huh.

It is one thing for the victim to forgive the person who tried to have him killed. It even makes a strange kind of sense for the victim to offer a sort of moral support over the phone. But for the victim to offer amateur legal counsel to the person who plotted to kill him—and for the accused to accept it—is breathtakingly bizarre.

It may also have been a terrible mistake for Danton. Frost told him how to act, what to say, how to plead. Though he claimed to be on the phone every day to help coach Danton through a tough moment, it has to be kept in mind that the result of Frost's help was a felony conviction and several years behind bars. Supposedly there to offer support, Frost convinced Danton he couldn't win, that he had no case. Claiming to be there to help clear Danton's name, Frost used his influence to urge his acolyte to admit his guilt. It is worth noting that the FBI had Danton's bumbling confession on tape anyway—a confession pried out of a bewildered Danton by the guy on the other end of the phone: Frost.

Was Frost working with the FBI to get Danton behind bars? It was at the FBI's request that Frost phone Danton in California—a call that he knew would be recorded. And on that call, he told Danton that the FBI had become aware of his murder-for-hire plot. It's also clear that he knew he was the target—he said so perfectly clearly. Pointing to himself as Danton's former coach on the Young Nats, and marvelling at the murder plot, Frost breathed into the phone: "God, you must have wanted that Nat guy gone, huh? Huh? Hey?" Is he coaxing Danton to confess on tape? Is he leveraging the player's trust to trick him into ratting himself out?

It is impossible to know. No one will ever know what the emotional entanglement is between the two men. Not even they could understand it. They are bound by a stifling, claustrophobic co-dependency, and darkness in their shared past, a blighted hope in their shared dreams—no doubt, a terrifying realization that they are bound together for life, that they really only have each other, as much as they might despise one another. Danton lived for Frost, yet wanted him dead. Is it difficult to believe that Frost wanted the best for Danton, but also wanted to see him behind bars?

Their relationship is a riddle, something that can never make sense. But as Danton languished in prison, that bond was a sickeningly powerful thing.

Frost: Hey Mike, listen, do I have to worry about my safety any more?

Danton: No you don't. I gotta go.

Frost: Okay, do you love me?

Danton: [whispers] Yes.

Frost: Say it.

Danton: I love you.

Frost: Do you?

Danton: Yeah.

14

Second Chances

The winds of winter swept across south-end Halifax's campus of Saint Mary's University in January of 2010, but the cold air must have felt like a rush of freedom to Mike Danton. This was, after five and half years behind bars, suddenly his new home, and, having exchanged his prison jumpsuit for jeans, a student's backpack filled with textbooks and a brand-new life, the twenty-nine-year-old Danton settled in nicely at the mid-sized institution with the motto, "One University. One World. Yours."

This was the place for new beginnings and second chances for Danton. It was a life he had never had, an education he had never had time for. And, as always, there was his first and most passionate love: hockey. After years in a jail cell, Danton would be back on the ice. Really, he couldn't have asked for anything more.

He had chosen to leave his home territory of Ontario, assuming he still had a place to call home, because he didn't want to be hounded by the press in Ontario, didn't want to be further poked or prodded by the media he mistrusted, wanted to start life anew. A new school. A new world to call his own. A new kind of freedom.

Really, it didn't take Danton very long to settle in at Saint Mary's, the first Roman Catholic–based university in Canada. From the beginning, he felt at home; felt a certain warmth through the coldest months on the Atlantic calendar; felt he could be himself in this new environment, maybe for the first time in his life, away from Dave Frost, away from his estranged family's surroundings, almost on his own as an adult. And what he never really counted on happened: he became something of a big man on campus.

At Saint Mary's, everybody knew his name before he attended his first class. He had been in the news for years. But at school, he became more than just another curiosity. He began to fit in with a student body so much younger than him. He wasn't being judged. He wasn't being pointed at. It was as if students went out of their way to befriend him, to help him, something he had never experienced before. His story may have been well known to those familiar with *the fifth estate* shows on his situation or the newspaper accounts from a few years earlier. But there was almost no student objection to an ex-con, a man who desperately attempted to arrange a murder, being among the fresh-faced young scholars in south Halifax.

None of this was guaranteed to happen. A lot of guys walk out of prison more bewildered than when they walked in. A lot of them are released back into the world they had been cut off from with no idea of what to do with themselves. Not many find themselves playing varsity sports, or walking from class to class at a respected university. And Danton didn't find his place there all on his own. Long before he arrived at Saint Mary's, he wrote to Trevor Stienburg, the long-time head coach of the university hockey team, asking if there might be a spot for him on the intercollegiate squad and inquiring about getting into school. His household name was still bandied about in Canada—and not in a good way. The coach wasn't certain what to think at first when he received the letter—out of the blue, a note from someone he knew of only from news headlines. That troubled kid from the troubled home with the troubling agent. No doubt, every student on campus knew who Danton was, and the players on Stienburg's nationally ranked hockey team certainly did. But the last thing the coach expected was a letter from the guy.

Still, in December 2009, Stienburg took the letter seriously enough to approach his hockey team. He gathered the group together before practice. "You're never going to believe who wants to play here," he told them. "Mike frickin' Danton."

"And then I laughed and sent them back on the ice." He figured that letter was the beginning of the matter, and also the end.

But Stienburg hadn't counted on Danton's famous tenacity. It turned out Danton didn't just write to the Huskies' coach—he began contacting some of the players as well. He didn't want to sneak up on anybody. He had jumped into teams at mid-season before and knew the kind of disruption a new player could bring with him. And he was smart enough to understand that he might not be welcomed with open arms. Throughout his career, Danton had been more outsider than insider on teams in St. Louis, in New Jersey, in Albany of the American Hockey League. He was usually the guy who didn't fit in, didn't make friends quickly or easily, didn't trust anybody, didn't play nice, wasn't part of the inside clique that seems to run most hockey teams from the dressing room on out.

Give Mike Danton credit. His overtures to the Huskies suggested the perennial outsider may have learned something from his mistakes.

Danton had spoken to Marc Rancourt, the captain of the Huskies, who was taken by his story, the potential comeback—and, of course, by what a former NHL player could bring to a collegiate team on so many levels. That, on its own, seemed enticing enough. Collegiate hockey teams in Canada are mostly composed of former junior players who all grew up with NHL aspirations but didn't have enough to play professional hockey. The thought of having an NHL player, and not just any NHL player, on the Saint Mary's team was exciting to the Huskies players. At first, that's one of the things that made Danton so attractive to them. He had been where every one of them wanted to go but would never get to—the NHL, not prison. He could be their window to what they would never know themselves.

Still, while there was plenty that Mike Danton could do for the players at Saint Mary's, they were in a position to give something back. Something anyone who had made a mistake might want, something anyone stepping out of prison hopes for: a chance to start over. "We have a unique opportunity here to provide Mike with a second chance that he has not only earned but is entitled to," Rancourt wrote in a letter to Stienburg. The letter was signed by every player on the Saint Mary's team, including those who thought they might lose their ice time, their spot on the dressed roster—and this team was expected to compete for the CIS (Canadian Interuniversity Sport) men's hockey championship.

But the final call on Danton belonged to Stienburg, the athletic department at Saint Mary's, and the university's admissions office. There were academic hurdles for Danton to clear as a mature student, and there was also the question of whether a twenty-nine-year-old former NHLer would be deemed eligible to play amateur hockey against collegians younger than his brother Tom.

Danton chose to try Saint Mary's first because he wanted to avoid attention, wanted to be away from mainstream media, but his story became national again and so were the steps that took him to Saint Mary's. Danton wasn't the first NHL player to go backwards and wind up playing university hockey, only the most famous. In the early 2000s, a player named Jared Aulin, a forward from Calgary, suited up for seventeen games with the Los Angeles Kings as a twenty-year-old and then returned to the University of Calgary to attend school and play hockey at the age of twenty-five. That didn't draw much attention at the time. This did.

What Danton probably didn't know when he tried to connect with Saint Mary's and Stienburg was that maybe he had identified not just the right program but the perfect coach for him and his situation. A lot of university coaches—a lot of coaches anywhere—would have received Danton's letter and tossed it in the garbage. Stars get second chances in pro sports. Fourth-liners don't usually get much help. Most coaches would have thought Danton wasn't worth the effort or the time or all the possible distractions that would come along with him. But Stienburg, drafted to the NHL in the first round of the same draft year that sent Mario Lemieux and Patrick Roy to stardom, had a certain feel for the type of hockey player Danton was, if not for the trouble he had been in for most of his life.

In fact, Stienburg's brief NHL career was surprisingly similar to Danton's—without similar endings, of course. Danton played 87 games in St. Louis and New Jersey; Stienburg played 71 games at forward, all for the Quebec Nordiques. Danton scored nine NHL goals; Stienburg scored seven. A rugged winger, Stienburg ended up with 12 career points but 161 penalty minutes; a rugged centre, Danton scored 14 points and had 182 penalty minutes. It would be almost impossible to find two players with statistics so eerily similar.

The real difference between the two, though, was upbringing: Stienburg grew up the son of a priest, a one-time prison chaplain who worked regularly with the National Parole Board. Stienburg had grown up around second chances, the most famous one being when the wrongly convicted murderer Steven Truscott lived in his home. If fate had set out to pick the perfect coach for Danton's second chance, Stienburg would surely have been at the top of a very short list.

"My dad said, 'Remember how you were brought up, son,'" Stienburg told *Sports Illustrated*. "He was like, if you take this kid, cover up, because you'll take some shots. But if you don't take him, don't let him rehabilitate, you'll have second thoughts.

"Initially, I was very hesitant. But I was challenged by my players for all the right reasons. I believe in second chances. And there's no question this was the right thing to do. He has paid the price for a mistake he's admitted was a huge mistake."

Once Danton was cleared to attend the university, then cleared athletically to play on the hockey team, Stienburg invoked one more rule: if David Frost is seen at a game, a practice, anywhere around campus, it's over. There was zero tolerance on this one. Stienburg was ready to give Danton the second chance his father always told him that everyone deserved. He was willing to do that but wanted no part of the Frost circus. He had heard all the stories and wanted nothing to do with Danton's mentor. Stienburg then went one step further—he invited Danton to live in his home, just as his father had done with Truscott and others years previously.

For at least the second time in Danton's life, he was living with his coach. But this time, no one was questioning the relationship in any way. The questions about Danton had little to do with his problematic past and everything to do with a former professional hockey player stepping back to the collegiate level and the ethical and competitive questions that went along with that.

The "shots" Stienburg's father had warned his son to protect himself from arrived just as he said they would. For Danton, there would be no hiding from the national media, even far from Ontario. Normally, Canadian university hockey gets almost no play in the mainstream media. Despite the fact that they were playing on one of the top CIS hockey teams in the country, the Huskies could have gone anywhere in the country in perfect anonymity. Stienburg could have added almost any player to his roster without raising an eyebrow. But Danton was not just another player. Suddenly, the issue of a twenty-nine-year-old NHL pro taking up a spot on a much younger university team had all sorts of media types screaming from coast to coast.

Among the most pointed critics was *Toronto Star* columnist Damien Cox, whose blog launched a withering attack on the Huskies' decision to allow Danton to suit up for them.

"The school claims it thought long and hard about this, and that Danton deserves a second chance. A second chance at what, exactly? A second chance at an education? Sure.

"But a second chance at hockey? Sorry, gentlemen, he's on about his ninth chance. He's a PROFESSIONAL hockey player. Surely that should erase eligibility to play university hockey in Canada, shouldn't it? Excuse my ignorance, but [how do] 161 games of pro hockey somehow make a player still able to play in the CIS …

"He's also 29 years old with a long rap sheet of misdemeanors and on-ice crimes. In junior hockey, he was a one-man wrecking crew, well, except for the times he was surrounded by the rest of David Frost's gang."

Cox devoted several paragraphs to voicing the same challenge that journalists and pundits were throwing at Saint Mary's. Was the school taking steps to keep Frost away from Danton? Had the school asked the ex-con any of the tough questions about what was going through his mind when he hired a hit man? Would anyone monitor his academic work, or was this just a cynical ploy to add some talent to the roster as Saint Mary's loaded up to take a run at a men's hockey championship?

The question of Danton's eligibility focused the spotlight uncomfortably on the whole CIS, as allegations arose that perhaps Canadian university hockey was not as different from the slick, sports-first-academics-later system south of the border. As Cox pointed out, varsity hockey teams are not filled with kids fresh out of high school looking to play sports when they go off to university—the rosters are full of guys on their own second chances, having already played major junior. People loved the feel-good story of an ex-con turning a ruined life around, and onlookers were happy that Danton was going to school. But a lot of people had mixed feelings about seeing him take another kid's chance to play varsity hockey so that he could have another shot.

The debate raged on nationally, in columns and on radio call-in shows. Some parents of university-aged hockey players raised a small fuss, but little came from Saint Mary's at all. The players, even those losing their ice time, seemed fine with Danton coming on board. And over time, the controversy waned, becoming yesterday's news. The university admitted Danton. For all the heated conversation in the media, there was no rule preventing him from playing university hockey.

The first year for Danton at Saint Mary's proved to be nearly magical. Danton took to school with the same kind of verve and passion with which he took to hockey. He wasn't going to allow himself to be cheated athletically or academically. He spent so much time in the campus library studying, it seemed like the place was his second home.

On the ice, Danton became the kind of popular teammate he never was as a professional or a junior, the wise old veteran instead of the wise-ass kid. He had been to the NHL, played in the Stanley Cup playoffs, been a contributor on the St. Louis Blues, and earned more than $500,000 in a season. He may not have been the biggest star on the Blues, but he was certainly the marquee player on the Huskies. His teammates would gather around him, ask questions, joke with him, and try to get a little of his veteran magic to rub off on them. While he never returned to the kind of form that saw him scoring a Stanley Cup playoff goal, Danton had a huge impact on the team. The kid who had always made his teammates a little uncomfortable somehow brought the Huskies closer together. He played just seven games for Saint Mary's on their way to a CIS championship, scoring three goals and setting the tempo in many games with his relentless pursuit of the puck. That had not disappeared in his time away from the game. The energy was still there, even if the hands and the legs weren't the same any more.

And in his first season with Saint Mary's, really a half-season for Danton, who was less than a year out of prison, the Huskies won their first and only men's national title. Danton had scored two goals in the Atlantic finals win over St. Francis Xavier and played a large role in the weekend CIS championship tournament in Thunder Bay. This, he would later recall, was the highlight of his hockey career.

"He's been unreal," Stienburg, the coach, said of Danton after the overtime victory against Alberta in the championship game. "The city, the school, and the team have embraced him. Maritimers love him. This has been an incredible story."

The response by Danton post-game was heartfelt and emotional. He wasn't anything like this after winning the Ontario Hockey League finals. The comeback story just kept getting better. "This is six years of waiting," Danton shouted with glee in a post-game televised interview. "This is for everybody who supported me, prior to my incarceration, during my incarceration, and everybody that embraced me afterwards. This is for everybody back home in Halifax, in Ontario, everybody that's supported me everywhere.

"This is special, this is for everybody!" he screamed. "For all the guys on our team, the whole community, it's wonderful. It's beautiful." This was the "happily ever after" the "once upon a time" began, but it may end up being the last great hockey moment of Danton's life.

The first year at Saint Mary's was storybook-like. The second season was less newsworthy. If Danton hoped to one day move back to professional hockey, to use this hockey experience to begin another professional assault, then at the advanced age of thirty, there was little in his second season indicating that would be possible.

He played twenty-eight games for the Huskies, scored the same number of goals, three, as he did in seven games the year before. He ended up almost last on the team in scoring, last in the plus–minus category, statistically leaving little indication that he could ever be a pro that mattered again. But off the ice, things were going much better. Danton had a steady girlfriend, a heavy workload, and then came the honour that perhaps best marked his time at Saint Mary's. Winning the national championship was wonderful, especially at a university that heavily stresses athletics, but being named an academic all-Canadian for maintaining an A average as a psychology major while playing CIS hockey was a tribute to all the work he had done.

In less than two years, convicted felon Mike Danton had gone from the gritty world of a life behind bars to the ivy-covered colonnades of a prestigious university. He had bounced back from the notoriety of his crime and the invasions of the media microscope to become a national champion. He had recovered from a disastrous decision to earn academic acclaim. At a glance, Mike Danton would seem to be proof of the possibility of rehabilitation.

At a glance, he would look like a poster boy for second chances.

Mike Danton deserves a lot of credit for turning his life around, no doubt about it. And Trevor Stienburg deserves his share of credit as well—without his generosity and willingness to take a risk, Danton's second chance would never have happened. But the fact that the ex-con's fate ended up in the hands of a hockey coach at all is a hint that there were three people who went unacknowledged when Mike Danton claimed exuberantly that the Huskies' championship was for "everyone." What he seemed to mean was "everyone but my parents and brother."

Hockey players almost always thank their parents when they win something. When even a grizzled old veteran lifts the Stanley Cup, he tends to take a moment to thank his mother and father for all the cold mornings spent at the rink, all the miles put on the car while driving to and from umpteen rinks, all the tournaments and hockey schools and new sticks and skates. Behind every hockey player, whether he or she is successful or not, there are parents who have invested immensely in both time and money. And Steve and Sue Jefferson invested more than most. If they hadn't, if they had not done what it takes to help a kid become an elite hockey player, their son would not have been the big man on campus when he was released from prison. He wouldn't have been on campus at all. They may not have been perfect, but without the first chance they gave their son, there would have been no second chance.

So when Danton was making headlines again, while he was heading back to school, travelling to yet another hockey tournament under the spotlight, Steve and Sue Jefferson watched with the kind of breathless worry and hope that all mothers and fathers go through.

And they suffered a kind of worry and hope that other parents are spared. They weren't just cheering for their son. They were hoping against hope, as they had been for years, just to see him again.

But even as Mike Danton's life began to turn around, he has been further removed from his family's life than ever before.

Somehow, even when things were looking up for the reformed scholar, something has kept him shackled to the past. As a psychology major with an A average, Danton might be expected to have some kind of insight into the workings of his own mind and his own memory. But while he may have become adept at understanding others, he seems to have remained completely blind to what was going on in his own life. And there is an inconvenient reality check that will not go away.

That reality check calls into question the entire life that Mike Danton has built for himself. It challenges his claims that he has changed, that his remorse has shown him how to live his life better, that he has learned from his mistakes.

Why? Because Mike Danton will not even acknowledge what his mistake was.

At his September 2009 National Parole Board hearing, board member Michael Crowley asked Danton to recount the crime he pleaded guilty to. Danton surprised everyone by saying that he had tried to arrange an assassination, not of David Frost, but of his father, Steve Jefferson.

"Are you sitting here today saying David Frost was not the intended victim?" Crowley asked in the board hearing.

"Not my intended victim," Danton replied matter-of-factly.

"I'm having a hard time believing this, to be truthful," Crowley told Danton. "There has to be more than what you just told the board."

Danton then went on to explain that he thought a hit man was coming from Canada to kill him. "Over the years, there were conversations that pointed to someone who would have interest in ending my life, ending Dave's life," said Danton. Danton even said he had "verbal confirmation" from a family member that heightened the fear.

Never mind the logic of this, that he had told two different prospective hit men that the person he wanted "taken care of" was living in his apartment in St. Louis at the time that Frost was living in his apartment. Never mind that he had given a photograph of Frost to one of the people he was trying to hire and indicated he was to be the target of the assassination. Never mind that Steve Jefferson had never been there, had never even visited St. Louis or spoken with Danton in years. Never mind that Frost had already acknowledged that he knew he was the victim. What Danton was telling the board could not possibly have made sense.

Danton's lawyer stood up and indicated at the parole board hearing that this was difficult to discuss in the presence of reporters.

The inconsistencies would be discussed behind closed doors. The board agreed to a short break to discuss the matter without reporters present, then returned to an open setting and Danton continued with his story about wanting his father dead.

"It's clear you thought it was your father," Crowley said.

"Right," Danton said, and went on to heap insults on his father, complain about his upbringing, and level allegations of "chronic abuse" growing up.

"It didn't matter if I had played a good game or a poor game," he claimed before the board. "The end result was the same. There was going to be a beating.

"… I just wanted to get rid of the thing causing me paranoia," said Danton. "I obviously wasn't thinking clearly."

What was said during the recess can only be guessed at. The National Parole Board, however, bought the Danton story, hook, line, and sinker, and Danton was released from the Pittsburgh Institute, just outside of Kingston, Ontario. On the way out of the hearing, a group of reporters waited for Crowley, trying to comprehend his decision and how he bought Danton's version of the truth. Among the conditions of parole: no contact with his father. He was allowed telephone contact with Frost.

"I'm sorry," Crowley said to the reporters outside. "We don't answer questions." Apparently, they don't ask them very well either.

But Norm Smith, who was the chief lawyer in the criminal section of the United States Attorney's Office in the southern district of Illinois, didn't buy Danton's story. He had worked on the case himself. He told *Maclean's* magazine that Danton's version of events was "flat out goofy."

"I can tell you this makes no sense," said the guy who knew the case against Danton better than anyone. According to Smith,

Danton broke down sobbing while being interviewed by FBI investigators at the time of his arrest, admitting that Frost was the intended victim, and he came unhinged by his fear that Frost "was going to leave him."

"Some things," *Maclean's* wrote of Danton's parole, "defy explanation."

To date, Danton has not changed his tune. Even as he goes through the poses of his new life, Danton has maintained that his father was the intended target of his bungled hit—even though every conceivable piece of evidence points to the contrary. He repeated the same claims in his nationally televised interview with former NHLer Nick Kypreos of Sportsnet, a much promoted one-hour television special. Danton later did similar interviews with the U.S. media giants *Sports Illustrated* and ESPN. His story was a natural for the big boys of the media—the rollercoaster tale of the hockey player with the bizarre upbringing who had gone to prison but is now on the comeback trail and getting straight A's at a venerable Canadian university. You couldn't invent this story if you tried, but Danton kept stretching the truth.

By the time Danton was talking to Sportsnet, the question was no longer "Why did you want your agent killed?" or even "Whom did you want killed?" Instead, Kypreos asked, "Why did you want your biological father killed?"

Through repetition, Danton had changed the question to suit his ready-made answers. Perhaps his training in psychology had helped him create his own spin. The story that worked with the parole board also worked with Sportsnet. So Danton stuck with it for *Sports Illustrated* and ESPN.

He has often told the story of his childhood, growing up in poverty. "The conditions of our house," he told Kypreos.

"Cockroaches, no toilet paper, no soap, no food, no clothes, no TV, no telephone … I didn't want the name Jefferson to be misconstrued with the person that I am."

There are numerous salient details, however, that he didn't tell Kypreos about in the Sportsnet interview. One of the homes he claimed was poverty stricken recently sold for $2 million—it had a swimming pool, and his dad made a skating rink every winter in the backyard. His family had a cottage in Muskoka. Strange that Danton claims the family didn't have food when the longtime business of both parents has been driving catering trucks. The Sportsnet interview would have been a lot more useful if Danton had been asked about any of these things.

Is Danton's assertion about who he was targeting in the botched hit a bald-faced lie? Sometimes, if you tell a story often enough, no matter how little truth there is to it, the story becomes yours after a while. It's no longer a lie. It's your truth, what you believe to be the truth, and Mike Danton made this his truth. It's not unlike the way Dave Frost planted stories in his head, repeating them ad nauseam, so that they became part of Danton's upbringing.

What all this seems to suggest is that Mike Danton has not escaped his past at all. He has not started the new life he claims to be leading. He has a new address, and some new friends, but he is still shackled to the same unbelievable stories that provoked him into committing a federal crime.

If he plotted murder in order to free himself from the constraints of the past, the only conclusion is that the failure of the plot means that he is still trapped. And if he is unwilling to admit the truth about the target of his attempt, that too indicates his unwillingness to go forth with his life.

Since leaving prison, he has been caught in a spiral of

self-destructive deceit. While he has found a comfortable home within the confines of the university world, he has yearned for a second chance in life and at a hockey career. That's what he wants most, what he pleads for in almost all of his interviews.

"I'm a good guy," Danton told Kypreos. "I don't want sympathy. I've made some mistakes; I've made some poor judgments.... And all I want is that second chance."

He wants that chance. It is a chance he has been unwilling to give to his family.

15

The Last Conversation

There was some kind of noise in the backyard. Or maybe it was just a mother's intuition. But Sue Jefferson found herself compelled to look out and see what the commotion behind her house was all about. And there she saw Tom, her baby, fourteen years old at the time, having just gone through the madness at David Frost's cottage and all that followed, already nursing a broken ankle from a hockey injury, cradling a case of beer. This wasn't just any underage teenager experimenting with drinking. When his mother saw him, he was so embarrassed, angry, emotional, and at wits' end that he hobbled off on his broken ankle, jumped the fence with one leg, and attempted to run away.

He didn't get very far.

"I was mad," says Sue, recalling the day. "I ran after him. It was clear something was wrong with him, I mean really wrong. When he got home, he starts heaving and heaving and then blood starts gushing from his mouth. It was horrible. It was frightening.

"I'm home alone. I don't have a car available. I don't know what to do so I call Dr. [Brian] Shaw [the NHL psychologist]. I said, 'Something's wrong with Tom. What should I do?'"

Tom turned to his mother and mumbled, "I just want to kill myself."

Tom talked a lot about having no reason to live after the horrors of his time at Frost's cottage. Sometimes he still talks that way. That day, he put back a toxic combination of booze and street drugs, figuring the combination just might end his life.

Steve raced home to drive his son to the hospital, figuring it would be faster than an ambulance.

"He was throwing up, all spun out of his mind, crying about his brother," said Steve Jefferson. "I think I ran red lights all the way to get him to the hospital. We knew what he'd been through but we didn't know what he was feeling inside. You can never know that. Once we got him to the hospital, they took care of him. He was okay.

"Okay, I think."

Almost all his life, Tom Jefferson has had difficulty escaping his brother's shadow, uniting with his brother, dealing with all of the family tumult that has been the Jeffersons' life. Everyone has been damaged here. But of all the victims, he is the most sympathetic figure, the least deserving of trouble, and maybe the most confused and confusing. He was just a little boy when his house was turned upside down. And he was just a boy of thirteen when he was introduced to the murky world of Dave Frost. Frost liked to tell people that Tom "was nothing but a little troublemaker." But no one asks for Frost's kind of introduction to manhood, his humiliating games of embarrassment. And from the time he left Frost's cottage, the two weeks that changed his life, Tom has fought all kinds of demons, tried to get his life on track, tried to find himself, almost always running into some kind of roadblock.

Like his father, Tom Jefferson can drink too much; and when he does, he can get himself into all kinds of trouble. He'll end up talking about his lost brother, his childhood idol; and the mental juxtaposition of how he can't live with him, can't live without him becomes prominent. Often, he can't stop talking about Mike, and yet he can't stand it when all of the family talk is about his older brother.

"Steve watches his hockey, goes fishing, drinks, cuts the lawn," says Sue Jefferson. "He really doesn't want to talk. He's really been hurt by the way Mike talks about the family. Steve can bury himself in other things and forget, at least sometimes for a few minutes. Tom hasn't been able to forget or forgive. It's been very hard for him."

"At fourteen, I was smoking," says Tom. "I was taking cigarettes from my dad's truck and stealing change throughout the week so I could go out and get a twelve-pack and get hammered with my buddies. Over time, I wish I never did that. It didn't do much for my mental state … didn't help me at all."

There are two things to know about Tom Jefferson. One, he has an inner strength the rest of his family may be lacking. He demonstrated it at age thirteen, at Frost's cottage, when it might have been so easy to align himself with his brother. He could easily have become one of them, the way Adam Keefe, Sheldon's younger brother, became one of them. Others might have given in or given up. Especially one so young. But he refused to give in.

And two, he doesn't share his brother's opinion or Frost's opinion of his parents and their home. He still lives with his parents at the age of twenty-four. Clearly, he loves them. He supports them. He understands they have flaws and weaknesses. He understands their hurt and he's not about to abandon them. In so many ways, they need him and he needs them. Difficult as that sometimes can be.

In 2002, when it became known that older brother Mike changed his family name to Danton, officially distancing himself from his family, Tom Jefferson did not take it well. Like so much of what had happened with his family, he didn't understand. He believed in his parents, in his home, in his upbringing however flawed it may have been. But amid all his personal demons and difficulties, he has remained loyal to his family and wanted to prove that to his parents.

And at the age of fifteen, without telling anyone and before it was legal to do so, Tom took the Christmas money that his grandmother had given him that year, took a bus and a commuter train from their Brampton home to faraway downtown Toronto, all in order to have a tattoo emblazoned on his arm. In large letters, running almost from shoulder to elbow, he had "Jefferson" indelibly written on his arm.

"I'll never change my name," he told his mother. "They'll have to cut off my arm to do it."

"That made me cry," says Sue Jefferson. "He was deeply affected by Mike changing his name, but we didn't realize how much so until this.

"When he showed the tattoo to Steve, he was so touched by it that he wanted to get the same tattoo on his arm. It meant that much to us."

"I just started bawling when he showed me," said Steve. "At first, he was afraid to show us. But once he did, I just lost it emotionally. I was so proud of him for doing that and every time I tell the story to someone, I start crying all over again."

How many fifteen-year-olds, having been through what he'd been through, would have summoned the courage to make that kind of personal statement, to see the pain his parents were suffering and do what he could to soothe it? He had that strength but he also has a Jefferson side to him. He has the self-destructive side that has damaged Mike, Steve, and himself on various occasions.

"I was fourteen when Mike changed his name," said Tom. "I thought that really sucked. I didn't know why he did it. My parents were quite upset and I wanted to let them know I wasn't about to do the same thing. I'm a different person from my brother, but I don't think I'm that different. I just think that he was caught. He said there was no love in our house and we lived in squalor. There was love. I felt love. I've had friends who lived in squalor. We didn't live in squalor. I didn't understand what he was doing, what he was talking about. I didn't understand, but I still wanted him back. It's always been that way."

Just like Mike, Tom Jefferson might have been a professional hockey player, too. He had similar talent to his brother—he played in the Ontario Hockey League—but maybe not similar intensity or focus. He was, according to trusted hockey scouts, a skater of professional quality who may have lacked the dedication, desire, or concentration to take the next step available to him. It is that difficult to advance from junior hockey to the professional game.

"As an athlete, he had everything but hands," says Brad Selwood, the former NHL player who traded for Tom while he was general manager of the OHL's Oshawa Generals in 2004. "He was a little tank who could skate like the wind. If all the other stuff wasn't going on, who knows what might have happened with him. But if his brother made it to the NHL, playing the role of the pesky player, I honestly believe Tom could have made it, too."

Selwood believed in Tom probably more than Tom believed in Tom. And because he believed in him, and felt something for his troubles, he gave Tom opportunity after opportunity to make it in junior hockey. It didn't work out that way. Tom ended up playing only 46 games for the Oshawa Generals before being released, but during his Generals stint, he and Selwood developed an unusually close relationship for a player and his general manager. At the time, Tom clearly needed an authority figure outside of his home to trust.

"Tommy sat in my office one day at the Civic Auditorium and started telling me about things that happened to him," says Selwood. "At first, I didn't know what to think. I didn't know if this stuff was in my head or whether it was real. He confided in me and told me a lot and often he'd break down in the middle of our conversations. At first you don't know what to believe, but when you see how he reacts, you know what's going on. All that happened to him sure took its toll on Tom. I quickly came to realize that everything he was telling me was true.

"He would come to my office quite often and I wanted to make him feel, the way I want all our players to feel, that they can tell me anything. He was dying to confide in somebody. You could see that. He often talked about killing himself, saying he just wanted to end it. He couldn't talk about a whole lot of anything else, other than what happened to him. I wound up calling [OHL commissioner] Dave Branch and I told him a little about what was going on. He put me in touch with a psychologist from the NHL. Tom was a troubled kid; we were doing our best to help him."

And always, Tom spoke of his brother Mike, but never in a negative way, even after all that had happened. "You could see he idolized Mike," says Selwood. "You could see how important it was for his family to get back together."

He would talk earnestly with Selwood, and then mess up after the conversations. That was the pattern. Late for curfew. Late for meetings. Seemingly irresponsible. School issues. Complaints from his billet. Tom wanted to behave: he just didn't know how. "I had so many issues with him away from the rink. I kept giving him a couple more chances. And a couple more after that. Then I couldn't give him any more.

"I finally called him in and told him I'd given him one or two more chances than I should have. I told him he was becoming a distraction. I felt really badly for him. I told him, 'I can't help you if you don't let me.' I'd reach out and then he would skip curfew the next night or there would be some incident. It wasn't any one thing with Tom. It was just too many things."

Tom Jefferson was released in 2005 by the Oshawa Generals at the age of seventeen. He would go on to play two more games in the OHL for the Barrie Colts. His NHL dream, if ever there was one, ended before his eighteenth birthday.

"Brad knew I was drinking and I think he knew I was a mess," said Tom. "I look back and realize I screwed up. I had too many things going on [in my head]. It wasn't until everything slowed down and everything stopped that I realized how badly I screwed things up."

But before he left the OHL for good, Tom left an impression of sorts from his involvement in an on-ice incident that got the attention of most of junior hockey. The Oshawa Generals were scheduled to play the Kitchener Rangers in December of 2004. Long before the game, some threats started getting to Tom Jefferson; they were not-so-quiet threats coming from Adam Keefe, younger brother of Sheldon and still a member of the Frost entourage. Before the game was ever played, Tom went to Brad Selwood and told him that Keefe had threatened to kill him. Intimidation in hockey at this level is part of the experience. Most of it is meaningless talk. But because it was Keefe, and because of the background of Frost, Selwood took the threats seriously.

"Tom said he wasn't sure if he should play or not, in fairness to the team and all," said Selwood. "In the end, he decided to play and I think it was the right decision. I figured, Keefe was a fifth-year kid, playing on a first line in Kitchener and Tom was a third- or fourth-liner on our team. Really, how much would they see of each other on the ice? That said, I did make sure to inform the league what was going on. I talked to Mr. Branch about it. I just wanted to make sure the league was aware of it."

Before the game, the coaches on both teams were made aware of the potential problem, and essentially warned about it. "And that's what pissed me off about what happened. The coaches knew what was going on, and I think Peter DeBoer [the Rangers coach, who has since made the jump to the NHL and was fired as coach of the Florida Panthers after the 2010–11 season] chose to ignore the [warning]."

Late in the game, the Kitchener Rangers made a line change of just one player and Keefe came on the ice to line up against Tom. Within seconds after the puck dropped, the rookie Tom was fighting the veteran Keefe. According to DeBoer, Tom provoked Keefe to fight "by yapping all night long."

"That's his view," said Selwood. "I don't agree with it. I guess Peter's memory of what happened and mine are pretty different."

According to Selwood, Keefe "just pounded on him and literally stood over him and pounded on Tom. To be honest, I was a little pissed off at our coach [Bob McGill] and a little pissed at the guys on the ice. Nobody jumped in to break it up. Nobody supported him. Tom was overmatched. He got pounded by Keefe and I wanted somebody to get in there. Do I think that fight was orchestrated? Absolutely. Do I think [Dave] Frost was behind it? Absolutely, even though I have no proof of it. It's just the way I feel."

Fighting has become an outlet of sorts for Tom Jefferson, especially now that he doesn't have the luxury of being able to do it within the confines of a hockey rink. Junior hockey breeds young fighters. For those who stay in the game at the professional level, there has always been a place for fighters. But Tom left hockey before he wanted to—essentially, he was told to leave—and, too often, he would carry the fighting game with him off the ice.

Looking back, Tom figures the fight with Keefe was just a follow-up to everything that had gone on at Frost's cottage. Keefe was instructed, or acted on his own, to take a piece of Tom Jefferson because of the attention he had brought to Frost and the boys by taking his case to the police.

"Every time we saw each other, he either had no respect for me, or maybe he was embarrassed by what happened at the cottage," said Tom. "My brother always said I shouldn't have said what I said. He said that's all lies and you know it. I said to him, 'How can it be lies? I was there.' And it gets you confused. He said, 'You're just a little troublemaker. You're just listening to Mom and Dad.' And I always thought, 'What the fuck is wrong with him?'"

Now in his early twenties, Tom Jefferson makes a decent living as a carpenter working for a major construction company in the Toronto area. And in these times of economic uncertainty, he doesn't necessarily have to worry about finances. That may be all he doesn't have to worry about. He is introspective and troubled and bothered by how he feels.

"I feel like I've changed and not for the better, for the worse," says Tom. "I don't have patience to listen to anybody. I don't have the time of day for it. Sometimes, someone is talking to me and I'm not even listening. I just tune them out. It's like, 'I don't care about you, I've got my own problems.'

"And sometimes, the more I think about it, the more negative a person I can become, the more destructive. I can't trust people. I don't trust people. And when I tell someone about what happened, you feel okay when you're saying it, and afterwards all it does is bring back memories. And that puts me in a fucked-up mood. It doesn't do any good for me.

"People have said, 'Get help,' but I just think it's a fucking waste of time. I know why I have these feelings. I know why I'm mistrusting. I know that I'm OCD [obsessive-compulsive disorder]. You know what would make me feel better? If my brother and I would start speaking again and if Frost was dead. That's the thing. I think I understand what Mike was doing when he tried to kill him. That part I understand. He was trying to change his life and that was his way of doing it.

"At the cottage, Mike didn't stand up for me once. And you wonder, how did he live with himself after that? How did that make him feel? I know how it made me feel. That's why I have trust issues with just about everybody around me. I tell my friends I can't trust them. I've told my girlfriend I can't trust her. I haven't dealt with this; it's kind of ruined my life.

"David Frost has fucked up my family, destroyed it beyond fixing. Sometimes, I don't know where I belong. I don't want to be at work. I don't want to come home. I don't know where to go. I get in my house and I'm immediately on edge. I kind of just want to go away, go away and start all over again. But I can't. I feel like I'm stuck. And I don't want to talk about this any more."

The last time any member of the Jefferson family spoke with Mike Danton happened quite accidentally. Not surprisingly, it occurred at an arena.

Tom Jefferson, finished with competitive hockey himself, still plays the game on occasion. He was participating in a union hockey tournament on a fall day in 2009, not long after his older brother had been paroled from the Canadian prison system. He finished his game that day, showered, and figured he would head home. What he never figured on was running into his brother after so many years.

Just out of jail, searching for redemption, and hoping for a return to competitive hockey, Mike Danton was trying to get his legs back, skating at the Mississauga Iceland complex. Tom was skating on one rink in the complex; Mike was skating on another.

With his bag flung over a shoulder and his sticks in hand, Tom was walking out of the arena, not thinking about anything in particular, when suddenly he stopped and stared, transfixed by what was ahead of him. There sat his brother. What had it been, a decade maybe?

Mike was sitting on the floor, with his hockey bag beside him, with buds in both ears, listening to music.

"I did a double-take," said Tom. "It was like, 'What's going on here?' I hadn't seen him since I was thirteen. My mind was racing. My heart was racing. I was almost in a daze. I knew it was him. I was shocked, surprised, excited."

So surprised he didn't know what to do. He walked to his car, put his equipment in the back, and slowly made his way back to the arena, feeling a mix of excitement and trepidation. "My heart," he said, "was pounding."

He made his way back into the rink to take another look at the brother he had once idolized; the brother who had rejected the family name only to have his adopted name splashed all over the newspapers; the brother who had turned their lives upside down.

Mike was sitting in the food area when Tom got back inside.

"I noticed him. He didn't notice me," said Tom. "I look a little different from when I was thirteen. He didn't know who I was. When I walked back into the rink he was still sitting, listening to his headphones, not really paying attention to anybody, kind of eyes half open.

"So I sat down at one of those little square tables opposite him, pretty close to him so he couldn't not see me. And I looked at him and I kept looking at him and when he saw me, I gave him one of those little friendly nods you give people you don't necessarily know. Like, hey, how's it going? He took his ear buds out and said, 'What's up?' He gave me one of those nods back.

"I said, 'Hi, how are you?'

"He just looked at me, looked at my face and I don't know how long it was, but it seemed like it was for the longest time. He didn't put it together. He didn't know who I was. Finally, it must have hit him."

The first words between two estranged brothers in almost a lifetime apart were hardly what Tom Jefferson was hoping to hear.

"I can't talk to you," Mike Danton said, shocking his brother once again.

"What do you mean? What do you mean you can't talk to me?" said Tom.

"I can't fucking talk to you," Mike Danton said.

"I was stunned," Tom recalled. "I couldn't believe he was saying this."

"Don't talk to me," said Mike. "Thank Steve for this. Thank your father."

One of the conditions of Mike Danton's parole was he couldn't have any contact with his father. But there was no condition prohibiting contact with his brother.

"Are you serious?!" Tom Jefferson shouted. "Are you serious?"

Mike was clearly getting antsy, nervous, looking around as though he was being watched or something. Tom was so excited by the discovery but emotions between the brothers were rarely similar. Mike was clearly irritated, not sure what to do. "He was putting his stuff in his bag, putting his headset away, looking around, very uncomfortable like," said Tom.

When Mike Danton stood to leave, Tom stood as well. He opened his arms, inviting a hug he had spent years waiting for, a gesture he hoped would keep his long-lost brother from slipping away again.

Mike Danton backed away from his brother.

"What the fuck?" Tom said.

"You can thank Steve for this," Mike repeated, as though he had nothing else to say. He got up and walked away.

"By this point, I'm pretty much breaking down, inside and out," said Tom. "I didn't know what to think, what to feel. I'd waited so long for this. I walked in a circle, started to go one way and then walked the other way. We both left each other, each of us walking in the wrong direction. We were clearly emotional, showing it in different ways. But each of us had to turn around and go the other way, not looking at each other.

"When he walked by me, I broke down in tears. I was crying and I was angry.

"I was telling him, 'I love you.'

"He knew. It's obvious. You know you're a little brother and you're supposed to look up to an older brother, even after all that's happened. It's only natural. It hurt to see he didn't give a shit. And after all that time, not speaking to him, not being able to spend all those years growing up with him, I expected more. I don't know why, but I did.

"It's pretty shocking to see that we're both at a mature point in our lives, but we couldn't get beyond the past. And I see by the interviews he's given that he's ready to mature and make a big change in his life. I've heard that, but I didn't get that from him. He had a chance to talk to somebody who loves him and he just walked away."

With tears running down his face, a confused and frustrated Tom Jefferson walked out of the Iceland complex on that fall day in 2009, but not before letting out his anger. He took his fist and pounded it into the glass arena sliding door, leaving significant damage behind. "The arena guy saw me," said Tom. "He had heard the confrontation. It was pretty loud.

"He just nodded at me, like saying, 'It's okay buddy. I saw it, I understand.'"

After he walked out the door, Tom felt he should have said more, done more, done something. He couldn't go. He walked back into the rink. Looked around. "By that time, he was gone."

Gone again.

"And I'm thinking, 'Where are you? Why don't you stay here and talk to me. We have a lot of things to talk about.' At the same time, I wanted to grab him and smack him, just something to wake him up, make him realize I wanted to talk to him. It was a coincidence we ran into each other. I wanted to say more. I wanted it to be more."

The last words from Tom Jefferson to his older brother, Mike Danton: "I love you."

The shattered glass of an arena door, with cracks in all directions: The Jefferson family mural. In the beginning and in the end, it always came back to hockey.

Mike Danton remains estranged from his parents and brother. According to sources, he keeps in regular contact with Dave Frost. He lived in Halifax, attended Saint Mary's University, and was a regular speaker at community functions. He has since hired an agent in an attempt to resurrect his pro hockey career. By publication time, he has not signed anywhere.

Dave Frost was discovered in 2010 working in the hockey business in California under the name of Jim McCauley. The hockey school he was associated with closed its doors and took down its website shortly after Frost's whereabouts were reported in the media. No longer an agent, Frost apparently splits his time between homes in California and a home in Georgetown, Ontario.

Upon his retirement from hockey, **Sheldon Keefe** became coach, general manager, and governor/owner of the Pembroke Lumber Kings, one of the more successful tier-two junior hockey operations in Canada. The Lumber Kings won the national tier-two championship in 2011. His assistant coach is Shawn Cation. While it has never been proven, there was word around hockey circles that both Frost and Mike Danton had pieces of the Pembroke team as well, but Frost has been banished from any contact with the team by the governing body of that junior hockey league.

Steve Jefferson continues to work in the catering business and lives with his wife, **Sue**, and son, **Tom**, just northwest of Toronto. Sue has chosen not to return to work. Tom works in the construction industry for a well-known company. All three Jeffersons still hope to be reunited with Mike Danton someday.

Bob Goodenow was forced to resign as executive director of the NHL Players' Association on July 28, 2005, after thirteen years in the prestigious position. He received a multi-million-dollar buyout for his time. Goodenow spends most of his time in Tequesta, Florida.

ACKNOWLEDGMENTS

On January 11, 1999, in a small item of sports news, the St. Michael's Majors of the Ontario Hockey League traded their best players to the Barrie Colts.

Normally, I don't pay very much attention to junior hockey, but this somehow struck a chord with me. Something seemed wrong about it.

"Why," I asked Terry Koshan, then the junior hockey reporter with the *Toronto Sun*, "would a last-place team trade their best players away?"

Koshan didn't hesitate in answering: "Because they want to get away from Frost," he said.

"Who's Frost?" I asked.

"You don't want to know," he answered.

That brief conversation, more than a decade ago, never left me. That day, I made some phone calls, did some asking around, and around dinner time filed a column on David Frost and the trading away of the Majors stars, including leading scorers Sheldon Keefe and Mike Jefferson. The editor putting out the sports section that night, John Kryk, read the column and called me over to his desk.

"We can run this if you want to," he said. "But I don't think you have the story. I'd rather hold this and go get the story."

The column never ran that day—the first and only time I've had a column spiked in my career—and about a month or so later, after numerous interviews and more than my share of telephone hang-ups and rejections, I wrote the first real exposé of the junior-hockey manipulator, Frost.

I didn't think I'd still be writing about him twelve years later. But the story wasn't simply about one man or junior hockey: In fact, there has never been a hockey story like this, if this is in fact a hockey story at all. As the years passed, the branches on the trees grew more and more entangled. The story became about lives ruined, dreams destroyed, families divided, careers cut short, and eventually an attempted murder and prison time.

This is a terrible yet important story—and one that needed to be told in full.

The story is about Mike Danton and his family, but Danton was never interviewed in preparation for the book. Emails sent to his address at Saint Mary's University were never returned or answered. Still estranged from his family, he has made some public proclamations about his family and his hockey life since being paroled from prison and before, but almost all of them ring untrue. Frost was not approached either to verify the stories told about him. His history for deception is deep and detailed. Nothing he has said could be considered credible or factual—but some of the material in the book was gathered from past interviews with him and court documents that include his testimony regarding his various legal entanglements.

This book could not have been written without the co-operation of the Jefferson family, Steve, Sue, and their youngest son, Tom. All three were generous with their time, forthright with their recollections, remarkably candid considering all that has gone on in their lives. They did not portray themselves as innocent in any way: In fact, no matter what the subject was, they answered every question asked, even the most painful ones. They opened up their hearts, their scrapbooks, their photo albums and legal papers, much of it troubling, all for the purpose of this book.

As someone who has been deeply involved in both minor hockey and family, I can't begin to imagine what their lives have been like. And it was that very motivation—and my belief in family—that got me interested in writing this story.

There is no hero in this story, but if anyone came across to me that way it was Tom Jefferson, a brave young man who has lived through a horrible ordeal. At thirteen, he could have easily become part of David Frost's inner circle. But even at that young age, he had enough strength and character to say no. I truly hope he finds peace in his life.

The research for this book included original interviews, almost one hundred in number, the use of secondary sources, and the reading and re-reading of police documents; court documents; newspaper, wire service, and website reports; and television documentaries.

Along the way, many have been helpful as interview subjects. Special thanks to hockey luminaries Lou Lamoriello, Larry Pleau, Joel Quenneville, Mike Kitchen, David Conte, the late Pat Burns, David Branch, Ron Wilson, Jay Feaster, Brad Selwood, Peter DeBoer, Bill Watters, Mike Futa, Mark Napier, and John Goodwin, among others, for their recollections.

And a large thank-you to the various levels of police who have helped along the way: From the FBI to the OPP to Peel Region to the Attorney General's Office in both Ontario and Missouri. Most of the officers, some retired, some still working, many in different jobs, would rather not have their names revealed here. They know who they are. Thanks again for the information.

Thanks also to the many good people at Penguin, starting with my editor, Nick Garrison. I handed him a sandwich, and he somehow turned it into—after several sound arguments—a full-fledged meal. It was a pleasure working with Nick. It was also a pleasure and a learning experience to work with my copy editor, Joe Zingrone. I wish I had him with me full-time. He cleaned up my work the way no one I have worked with before has managed. There are also a number of behind the scenes Penguin people I worked with by email or telephone conversation and never met. It took many people, including publicist Stephen Myers, to launch this project. I am grateful to everyone who helped carry me along.

Thanks, also, to whoever runs www.hockeydb.com—the resource, as it always is, was invaluable to me while I was accumulating information for this book and putting context to stories. Big thanks to Glenna Tapscott and Katherine Webb-Nelson of the *Toronto Sun* library staff, who helped out as they always do, with terrific enthusiasm and a remarkable ability to find things.

Some wonderful work on this subject has been done over the years in various formats: I would like to acknowledge the writing of Gare Joyce of espn.com; the excellent reportorial work of Greg MacArthur, then working for the *Ottawa Citizen*; the detailed reporting of junior-hockey writer Sunaya Sapurji, then of the *Toronto Star*; and the breakthrough documentary work of Oleh Rumak and Bob McKeown of CBC Television's *the fifth estate*.

Thanks also to many media friends and colleagues: John Kryk of the *Toronto Sun* for getting me started on this path; Terry Koshan of the *Toronto Sun* for his continued guidance and encouragement along the way; David Shoalts of *The Globe and Mail* for his friendship and writing on the subject; Christie Blatchford of the *Globe* and Rosie DiManno of the *Toronto Star* for their brilliant work on the sexual-exploitation trial of Frost and other related subjects; Allison Jones of the Canadian Press for her support, her meticulous reporting, and her terrific memory; Derek Goold of the *St. Louis Post-Dispatch* for his coverage of the murder-for-hire trial and his help whenever I needed it; Jeff Marek of *Hockey Night in Canada* and Sherry Bassin of the Erie Otters for their feedback and willingness to lend an opinion. Thanks to Steve Buffery of the *Toronto Sun* for making me laugh whenever I needed one throughout this difficult project. And special thanks to Bill Pierce, the sports editor of your dreams, my boss at the *Sun*, for encouraging the work beyond his pages and supporting my time away.

While many co-operated with me for this book, almost as many interview requests were declined or never responded to. That has always been the way, and the challenge, when writing about Mike Danton and Dave Frost. Front and centre among the many who declined to be interviewed or did not respond to inquiries: Sheldon Keefe, Bob Goodenow, Mike Gillis, NHL referee Wes McCauley (Bridget's brother), Larry Barron, Ryan Johnson, Brad Richards, Robert Haar, and Joey Goodenow.

Finally, this book is about a damaged family and how they lost their way. I am blessed to have the strength of my wife, Sheila, with me at all times, and the close loving relationships and friendships with my sons, Jeffrey and Michael. If anything, working on this has reinforced my belief in the value of family. Mine, I cherish— and I couldn't have completed this book without us being the unit we are.

A

Abid, Ramzi, 129

Aulin, Jared, 219

Anthony, Kenneth, 178

Avery, Sean, 124

B

Barnes, Ryan, 120, 123, 125, 148

Barnett, Mike, 110

Barron, Larry, 45, 48, 53, 105, 170-
172, 255

Bassin, Sherry, 130, 255

Batten, Don, 104

Benson, Chris, 41

Bettman, Gary, 114-115

Blatchford, Christie, 255

Bloom, Howard, 117

Branch, David, 38, 126-128, 130,
238, 253

Buffery, Steve, 255

Bure, Pavel, 108, 155

Burgess, Lee, 177-178

Burke, Brian, 108

Burns, Pat, 153, 253

C

Campbell, Ken, 178

Cation, Shawn, 105, 121-122, 125

Cherry, Don, 38

Ciccarelli, Dino, 39

Ciccarelli, Rob, 39

Coates, Al, 135

Coffey, Paul, 30

Conte, David, 117, 148-154, 160-
161, 253

Cox, Damien, 221-222

Crowley, Michael, 227, 228

Cunniff, John, 150-152

D

Daly, Bill, 114, 115

DeBoer, Peter, 121, 240, 253

Denis, Marc, 156
Dickson, Donald, 184
DiManno, Rosie, 27, 255
Dudley, Rick, 161

E
Eagleson, Alan, 108
Edelson, Michael, 47, 207, 209

F
Feaster, Jay, 161-165, 253
Ferris, Darren, 122-123
Frost, David, 2, 5, 7, 9-12, 16, 25,
    27-41, 44-60, 63, 65-66, 68-72,
    75-77, 79-84, 86-95, 97, 100-115,
    117, 120-126, 130, 138-140, 142-
    143, 147-149, 152, 155, 157-158,
    161-163, 165-169, 172-173, 175-
    176, 178-193, 197-213, 216, 220,
    227-228, 230, 233-236, 241-242,
    250-251, 253
Futa, Mike, 103-104, 119-125, 147-
    148

G
Gardner, Bonnie, 38-39
Gardner, John, 30
Garrison, Nick, 254
Gartner, Mike, 30
Gebe, Charlie, 65
Gebe, Luba, 65
Gebe, Susan (Jefferson), 72
Gillis, Mike, 106-109, 125, 139, 148,
    153, 154, 162, 255
Goodenow, Bob, 22, 24, 80, 99-117,
    161, 210, 250

Goodenow, Joey, 102-103, 105, 255
Goodwin, John, 37, 253
Goold, Derek, 255
Griffin, Geoffrey (Judge), 178, 189,
    191-193, 205

H
Haar, Robert, 195-197, 207, 209, 255
Hale, David, 149
Henein, Marie, 182, 186-187, 189-
    190
Holik, Bobby, 155
Hull, Brett, 102, 110
Hunter, Mark, 39

J
James, Graham, 39
Jefferson, Jeff, 134, 135, 139
Jefferson, Mike (also Mike Danton),
    1-24, 39-41, 43-45, 48-49, 51,
    55, 58-59, 61-71, 75-77, 79-80,
    82-94, 97, 99-109, 111-127,
    129, 131, 134-143, 147-162,
    164-167, 170, 174, 181, 189,
    194-213, 215-231, 242-246,
    249-251, 255
Jefferson, Steve, 2, 11-13, 17-24, 44-
    45, 53, 57-58, 64-66, 68, 70-73,
    75-77, 79, 80-97, 100-101, 103,
    105-107, 109, 111-114, 117, 122,
    134-141, 167-171, 173-175, 182,
    188-189, 192-193, 195-196, 210-
    211, 226, 234-237, 241-242, 244,
    250, 253
Jefferson, Sue, 18, 44-45, 53, 57, 59,
    61-74, 76-77, 79-80, 91-92, 97,

109, 117, 131, 137-138, 142, 167,
169-170, 173, 182, 184, 185,
188-189, 192, 194, 204, 226,
233-236, 241-242, 250, 253
Jefferson, Tom, 2, 43-60, 64-66,
68-70, 74-75, 77, 79, 86, 91, 97,
109-110, 116, 118, 175, 188, 194,
218, 233-246, 250-251, 253
Jiminez, John, 210
Johnson, Ryan, 204, 255
Jones, Allison, 255
Jones, Justin Levi, 9-15
Jones, Ronnie, 5-8
Joyce, Gare, 28, 254

K
Keefe, Adam, 50, 86, 171, 235, 239-
241
Keefe, Brian, 19, 59, 85, 136-137,
167-170
Keefe, Sheldon, 19-20, 48, 54-55, 59,
85-87, 104-105, 108-109, 119-21,
125-28, 143, 144-148, 161-165,
169, 172, 191, 239, 250-251,
255
Kilrea, Brian, 126
Kitchen, Mike, 206-207
Koshan, Terry, 251, 254
Kryk, John, 252, 254
Kypreos, Nick, 229-231

L
Ladds, Brent, 29
Lamoriello, Lou, 109, 149-150, 152-
154, 156-160, 165, 253
LaRoque, Ian, 183-184

Lecavalier, Vinny, 162
Lemieux, Mario, 219
Lindros, Eric, 30, 141

M
MacArthur, Greg, 254
Marek, Jeff, 95, 255
Martin, Paul, 149
McCauley, Bridget (Frost), 54, 75,
101, 166-167, 255
McCauley, Irene, 166-167
McCauley, John, 101, 166
McCauley, Wes, 166, 255
McGill, Bob, 240
McKeown, Bob, 9, 94, 254
Meehan, Don, 163
Messier, Mark, 155-156
Morgan, Chuck, 35
Morris, Pat, 165
Myers, Stephen, 254

N
Napier, Mark, 122-123, 125, 253
Naslund, Markus, 108
Naster, Jay, 179

O
Orr, Bobby, 122
Ovenden, Alec, 47

P
Passmore, Brian, 22-24
Penny, Ian, 110
Pierce, Bill, 255
Pleau, Larry, 4, 14, 112, 201,
253

Q

Quenneville, Joel, 63, 253
Quinn, Reg, 122, 125

R

Rancourt, Marc, 218
Richards, Brad, 131, 255
Richter, Mike 156
Rheaume, Pascal, 199-201
Rockwell, Norman 134, 138
Roy, Patrick, 219
Rumak, Oleh, 254
Rupp, Michael, 149
Rycroft, Mark, 202

S

Sapurji, Sunaya, 254
Saskin, Ted, 114-115
Scott, Richard, 37
Selwood, Brad, 237-240, 253
Shaw, Dr. Brian, 109, 116, 168, 210, 234
Shoalts, David, 171-172, 255
Skoula, Martin, 137
Slobodian, Michael, 72
Smith, Alex, 178

Smith, Gord, 40, 171
Smith, Norm, 228-229
Stephens, Charlie, 122, 123
Stewart, Bill, 125, 128
Stienburg, Trevor, 216-221, 224-225
Stiehl, William D., 195-196

T

Tapscott, Glenna, 254
Templeton, Bert, 125
Tiveron, Darryl, 33, 105
Tortorella, John, 162
Trevelyan, Tom, 95, 204-205
Truscott, Steven, 220
Tse, Sandy, 179, 182-85, 187, 191-192

W

Watters, Bill, 95, 174, 253
Webb-Nelson, Katherine, 254
Wirtz, Bill, 113-115
Wilson, Ron, 3, 253
Wolfmeyer, Katie, 8-15, 199

Y

Yzerman, Steve, 19-20